Christmas 2(

To Betty
from Stuart.

see back cover

Gross
Britain

Gross Britain

The Antidote to Patriotism

TAFFY ST GEORGE McSCOT

MICHAEL O'MARA BOOKS LIMITED

First published in Great Britain in 2005 by
Michael O'Mara Books Limited
9 Lion Yard, Tremadoc Road
London sw4 7nq

A CIP catalogue record for this book is available
from the British Library

isbn 1-84317-160-0

1 3 5 7 9 10 8 6 4 2

www.mombooks.com

Designed and typeset by Martin Bristow

Printed and bound in Germany
by GGP Media GmbH, Pößneck

Contents

CONTENTS - *continued*

> *'Britain will be honoured by historians more for the way she disposed of an empire than for the way in which she acquired it.'*
>
> LORD HARLECH

Introduction

A<small>T HEART, THE</small> B<small>RITISH ARE DEEPLY INSECURE</small>, and with good reason, too. Their country fell off the edge of mainland Europe during the last Ice Age and lost out on the best bits. This they have cleverly turned to their advantage, however, making incomparable virtues of smallness, mildness, and pleasantness. In a state of profound insecurity, they have delved into every corner of their island looking for some stray shard of true greatness – a rock, a fossil, a Roman pavement, a Saxon longship, a forgotten manuscript. They have built themselves up. They have puffed themselves out. They have convinced the whole world that Stonehenge is an extraordinary piece of architecture, that Christ Himself popped over for a ramble on their pastures green, and that the word 'great' in Great Britain is a reflection of sterling qualities. For a short period, they made the world take notice of them, and while they had the world's attention, they made it play their games, speak their language and accept Greenwich Mean Time as standard. Now the big balloon of the British Empire has popped, the air has rushed out, and there the country is all over again (but now minus a big chunk of Ireland), stuck out on its own in the sea, a bit crinkled around the edges.

Once the British had strange ideas about food, sex, sport, religion, the monarchy, law and order, the French, and what constituted a good education (flogging, mainly), but they had an empire, so who was to argue? Now they just have strange ideas. Like the hilarious one that some king or other had about uniting the countries of Scotland, England and Wales into one nation, and calling it *Great* Britain to distinguish it from Brittany across the water. And what about flying the red, white, and blue flag, and naming it the Union Jack? The man to blame for such apparent madness was James I of England, but hang on, wasn't he Scottish?

The dis-United Kingdom

IN 1603, WHEN KING JAMES VI of Scotland became James I of England, the two countries became united under the same monarchy, and three years later a new flag – the Union Jack or Union Flag – was introduced to honour and reflect this most unlikely of partnerships.

Over a hundred years later, in 1707, the United Kingdom of Great Britain was born. Since then, the Scottish have twice risen up against the English, Ireland joined the union for a bit (then bolted), and many an English-owned holiday cottage in Wales has mysteriously caught fire. The Land of Hope and Glory was on the march, its bounds being set wider and wider, but back in 'blighty', the business of bashing the Celts and sticking one in the eye of the English went on as ever. (Ironically, the word 'blighty' comes from an Urdu word meaning 'foreign' or 'European'. The British clearly have an aptitude for pinching words from other languages throughout the world.)

'When people say England,' said George Mikes, 'they sometimes mean Great Britain, sometimes the United Kingdom, sometimes the British Isles – but never England.' The difference between 'Britain', 'Great Britain', the 'UK', and the 'British Isles' is deeply confusing. In Northern Ireland, motor vehicles run around with 'GB' plates even though Northern Ireland has never been part of Great Britain.

St George, the dragon-slaying patron saint of England lived in Turkey in the fourth century and never set foot in England, but if England had had a problem with dragons around that time, no doubt St George would have been the man to sort it out. As it is, dragons have never posed a threat to England. Unless the dragon is Wales, with its dragon symbol. In that case, England's choice of patron saint seems in very poor taste.

After the rebellion of the Welsh prince Owen Glendower (from 1400 until about 1408), Henry IV enacted harsh laws against Welsh 'rimers, minstrels or vagabonds', whom he blamed for bad-mouthing the English in Wales. Rimers and vagabonds were all the same to him. The English king wanted Wales to be a bard-free zone, from which originates the native Anglo-Saxon aversion to Celtic folk singers, no doubt.

After the Norman Conquest of 1066, the Welsh border was entrusted to Norman 'Marcher Earls' with special powers to raise armies, build castles and enact laws. There is no record that the Earl of Chester's law forbidding Welshmen to 'enter the city before sunrise or stay after sunset on pain of decapitation' was ever repealed. Equally, in Hereford it is acceptable to shoot a Welshman with a bow and arrow under certain circumstances, according to the local statute books.

The word Wales comes from the Old English word 'Welsch' for foreigner. The native word for Wales is 'Cymru', meaning 'compatriots'. West of the River Tamar, Cornwall was 'Kerno' to the native Celts. The Anglo-Saxon invaders called the Cornish 'Kern-wealhas' – foreigners (again). To the English, foreigners will always be foreigners even in their own country.

> *'Cold-blooded queers with nasty complexions and terrible teeth who once conquered half the world, but still haven't figured out central heating. They warm their beers and chill their baths and boil all their food, including bread.'*
>
> The most salient characteristics of the English, described in *National Lampoon* magazine

In his 1755 *Dictionary of the English Language*, Samuel Johnson defined oats as 'a grain, which in England is generally given to horses, but in Scotland supports the people'. While touring the Scottish Highlands, he remarked to his London-based Scottish biographer, James Boswell, 'the noblest prospect which a Scotchman ever sees, is the high road that leads him to England.'

After the events of 1066, England found itself part of a glamorous European scene that was the height of civilization. New ideas about marriage, property, war and sex, and the saucy French language, once embraced, afforded the Anglo-Norman clergymen-scholars a new platform from which to hurl abuse at their Celtic neighbours. The Welsh, wrote Gerald de Barri, lived like beasts; they 'keep concubines as well as wives'. The Irish, said the classical scholar John of Salisbury, were so 'barbarous that they cannot be said to have any culture'. According to William of Newburgh, it was the Sunday sport of every Scotsman 'to cut the throats of old men, to slaughter little children, to rip open the bowels of women'.

❀

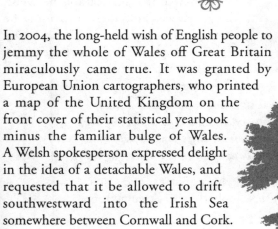

In 2004, the long-held wish of English people to jemmy the whole of Wales off Great Britain miraculously came true. It was granted by European Union cartographers, who printed a map of the United Kingdom on the front cover of their statistical yearbook minus the familiar bulge of Wales. A Welsh spokesperson expressed delight in the idea of a detachable Wales, and requested that it be allowed to drift southwestward into the Irish Sea somewhere between Cornwall and Cork.

'All Justices shall proclaim and keep all courts in the English Tongue . . . all Oaths shall be given in the English Tongue . . . no person or persons that use the Welsh Speech or Language shal have any office within this realm of England, Wales or other of the King's dominions . . . unless he or they use and exercise the English Speech or Language.' In the Acts of Union between England and Wales (1536–43), Henry VIII showed that his zeal for the Welsh language was boundless, providing he never had to listen to it. Today, many English people still maintain a Henrician regard for Welsh music.

> *'Taffy was a Welshman, Taffy was a thief;*
> *Taffy came to my house and stole a piece of beef:*
> *I went to Taffy's house, Taffy was not at home,*
> *Taffy came to my house and stole a marrow-bone.'*
>
> An old nursery rhyme popular in the 1950s
> among English schoolgirls with skipping ropes

> *'Sour, stingy, depressing beggars who parade around in schoolgirls' skirts with nothing on underneath. Their fumbled attempt at speaking the English language has been a source of amusement for centuries, and their idiot music has been dreaded by those not blessed with deafness for at least as long.'*
>
> *National Lampoon* magazine characterizes the Scottish

Halfway down the first page of *The Conqueror's Handbook*, after 'Intimidate the locals by building oversized castles' and 'Hound the rabble-rousers into the hills,' it says, 'Don't just be a great conqueror, be a great dad! Hand over your conquest to your son and heir along with the Second-Highest Title in the land.' Just so, having conquered Wales and wiped out the Welsh princes in the mountains of Snowdonia, Edward 'Longshanks' I formally made his sixteen-year-old son 'Prince of Wales' in a ceremony in Caernarfon Castle.

The original version of 'God Save the King' was written to boost the Hanoverian army in Scotland against the kilted Jacobites. It was later adopted as the British national anthem minus the less than inclusive last verse:

> God grant that Marshal Wade,
> May by thy mighty aid,
> Victory bring.
> May he sedition hush,
> And like a torrent rush,
> Rebellious Scots to crush:
> *God Save the King!*

Incidentally, Marshal Wade was a British field marshal and 'pacifier' of the Highlands. Being 'pacified' by the English, however, was not necessarily a process that other countries would have rushed to undergo.

> *'Ulster Protestants of Northern Ireland are a people chiefly characterizing themselves by what they are not, and neurotically undecided about what they actually are.'*
>
> W. HARVEY COX, on being an Ulster Protestant

To get a full head of bloom, the 'flower of Scotland' requires nothing short of the total humiliation of the English. Happily for them, the English tend to deliver at international sporting events:

> O flower of Scotland
> When will we see
> Your like again,
> That fought and died for
> Your wee bit hill and glen
> And stood against him
> Proud Edward's army
> And sent him homeward
> Tae think again.

The reference to 'proud Edward's army' concerns the shattering defeats of King Edward II's force by the Scots under Robert Bruce at Bannockburn in 1314. However, the song dates from a little later, having been written in the 1960s by the late Roy Williamson of The Corries.

The chorus of the national song of the Welsh, the anthem 'Land of My Fathers', speaks directly to Wales as if it were a person, as only a patriotic chorus can. It tells Wales it is not to worry, being doubly defended by the sea and the doughty Welsh heart. (The idea of the sea as a defensive moat has been a popular one with the English too. They also like to pretend they live on an island completely surrounded by water, despite England's borders with Wales and Scotland.)

> Wales! Wales! O but my heart is with you!
> As long as the sea
> Your bulwark shall be,
> To Cymru my heart shall be true.

William Blake's 'Jerusalem' is the only English hymn still capable of rousing church congregations to full voice. Belted out at the patriotic closing night of the Promenade Concerts at the Royal Albert Hall, it is the nearest an Englishman comes to believing that England is not only green and wholly pleasant, but also exactly the sort of place that the Son of God would visit for the pleasure of walking on the South Downs.

Britain has two well-known national songs, 'Rule, Britannia!' by Dr Thomas Arne and James Thomson, and 'Land of Hope and Glory' by Arthur Benson and Sir Edward Elgar. Both carry roughly the same message of a proud advancing nation. In 'Rule, Britannia!' Britain is shown to have emerged from the sea with one intention only, that of ruling the waves. Other nations would come and go, but not Britannia, says the

song, which would eventually rule the global seaboard ('And thine shall be the subject main, And every shore it circles thine.'). The Land of Hope and Glory would presumably sweep up the landlocked countries that missed out on the coastal rule of Britannia. ('Wider still and wider, Shall thy bounds be set; God, who made thee mighty, Make thee mightier yet.') Between Britain's two nationalistic anthems, nowhere is safe.

The only popular rituals celebrating Britishness in the British Isles are the Orange Parades of Northern Ireland, which are held on 12 July each year. Paradoxically, the rest of Britain looks on in total bafflement (and Irish Republicans in fury).

Alma Mater, Seed-Bed of Empire: British Education

AT ITS HEIGHT, THE BRITISH EMPIRE stretched over 11,400,000 square miles (18,350,000 square kilometres), comprising 410 million

subjects. Young bucks like Robert Clive grabbed it, looking for adventure, riches and multiple girlfriends. Old fogies like Cecil Rhodes justified it on the grounds that the British 'happen to be the best people in the world, with the highest ideals of decency and justice and liberty and peace'. It was only good manners to spread them around a bit. But who was going to run it? The British public schools patented 'Imperial Man', churning him out and packing him off to the colleges of Oxbridge – one of which aimed to instill 'the consciousness of Effortless Superiority'.

When Siegfried Sassoon arrived at Marlborough College as a young boy, his romantic imagination carried him on to the moment when the headmaster was bidding him goodbye at the end of his career. 'Well, Sassoon,' he would say, 'superlative scholastic ability isn't everything in the battle of life. Your sterling qualities of character have been an influence for good which I shall not readily forget. Thank you, my boy, I am proud of you.' In reality, however, the parting advice of his housemaster when the time came for Sassoon to leave was rather less appreciative: 'Try to be more sensible.'

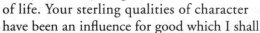

I see you were at the old place . . . Those were the days eh? . . . I don't suppose you'd remember old Tester (six months for indecent assault). I try to keep up with them. Whose house were you in?

Graham Greene reflects on his schooldays in *England Made Me* (1935). It was rumoured that the novelist found Oxford college life so tedious that he would take himself off into the countryside at night with a loaded revolver and play solitary games of Russian roulette.

The poet Percy Bysshe Shelley attended University College, Oxford for less than a year. He was expelled for 'contumaciously refusing to answer questions about the authorship' of a pamphlet entitled 'The Necessity of Atheism'. In 1891, the poet's daughter-in-law commissioned a statue for the British Cemetery in Rome of the naked, drowned poet swooning on a  marble slab while being mourned by the muse of poetry. When it proved too big for the Italian plot, she offered it to the poet's Alma Mater. University College's Old Boy was reinstated without a moment's thought.

A fag is gamely described in the *Guide to Eton* (1860) as 'a Lower Boy who performs some trifling offices for an Upper Boy, such as laying out his breakfast or tea; sometimes lighting his fire,' or – popular well into the twentieth century – warming his lavatory seat by sitting on it. At Winchester College, for the better performance of these 'trifling offices', juniors were made to hold burning brands to toughen their hands. The practice of 'roasting' was a torture particular to Rugby School, the bigger boys pinning a junior against the open fire until his trousers burned. 'Tunding' was Winchester jargon for a beating. (It is interesting to note that the motto of the centuries-old school is 'Manners Makyth Man'.) To this day at Tonbridge School, first-year pupils can be found hanging from coat hooks by their underpants, a practice fondly known as 'a wedgy'. 'There's been some bad work here,' mutters the housekeeper in *Tom Brown's Schooldays*, a Victorian novel set in – you guessed it – Rugby School. Indeed there has. Readers may care to note that parents pay very large sums to send their children to British public schools.

My dear mama, I wright to tell you I am very retched, and my chilblains is worse agen. I have not made any progress and I do not think I shall. I am very sorry to be such expense to you, but I do not think this schule is very good. One of the fells has taken the crown of my new hat for a target, he has burrowed my watch to make wheal, with the works, but it won' act . . . I think I have got the consumption the boys at the place are not gentlemen but of course you did not know that when you sent me hear, I will try not to get into bad habits . . .

Parents were advised to ignore cries for help in letters such as this one from a 'retched' Eton schoolboy. In an article on public school education in 1858, *The Times* concluded that 'Parents may well abstain from looking too closely into the process and content themselves with the result.'

That privately run, fee-paying schools are misleadingly known in Britain as 'public schools' confounds foreigners to the delight of the British. The term was originally coined by Eton College to differentiate between religious schools (which only members of the relevant denomination could attend) and those educational establishments that were open to all members of the paying public, hence 'public' school. For many centuries, aristocratic boys were privately educated at home. The increasing prestige of what were once grammar schools, like Eton, encouraged parents to send their boys away to be educated publicly, or as it was written in *The Times* in the reign of Queen Victoria, to 'melt the boys down and run them all out of the same mould like bullets'.

The man responsible for turning the Victorian public school into an engine of empire was Dr Thomas Arnold, the Headmaster of Rugby. 'Although our Saviour taught us to turn the other cheek,' he used to say, 'He did not mean that we were not to tackle our man low', which was a reference to rugby football, a sport invented at Rugby in the mid-nineteenth century when a boy named William Webb-Ellis picked up the ball and ran with it during a game of ordinary football. Arnold's disciples spread his creed of muscular Christianity throughout Victorian England, and thus out to the far corners of the Empire, though his talented protégé Charles John Vaughan's headmastership at Harrow came to an abrupt end when he tackled a handsome boy called Alfred Pretor a little *too* low. He ended his days as the Dean of Llandaff.

The public-school novel was Victorian Britain's special contribution to literature. It was these rose-tinted tales of life behind ivied walls that convinced otherwise sentient British parents to send their children away to boarding school:

1. Thomas Hughes's *Tom Brown's Schooldays* (1857) is set in Hughes's old school Rugby, where the eponymous hero Tom is notably duller at the end of his schooldays than at the beginning.

2. Sir Henry Newbolt's *The Twymans* (1912) takes place at Clifton, renamed Downton by Old Boy Newbolt. The heraldry-obsessed hero Percival's first impression of the school was 'the sweet crack of bat on ball'. Newbolt later seemed to be convinced that warfare was akin to a glorified cricket match.

3. Shane Leslie's *The Oppidan* introduced the reading public to the Eton slang for pupils boarding in town (*oppidum* is Latin for 'town'), while scholars boarding in College were simply 'Collegers'.

4. *Tim* by H. O. Sturgis (1891) is a novel in which the hero falls in love with a boy confusingly called Carol.

5. F. W. Farrar's *Eric, or Little By Little* tells of the gradual descent of the eponymous hero from small sins to great. He begins by laughing in church (for which he is flogged), and descends

to masturbation, which leads inexorably to 'shame and ruin, polluted affections and an early grave'. Farrar was an Anglican churchman much admired in his day, and his book about Eric was hugely popular.

6. In the *Harry Potter* series of novels, J. K. Rowling's stories of the fictional co-ed school of wizardry Hogwarts, one of the four school houses, Slytherin, uniquely specializes in evil.

H. E. Bates was convinced that at public school life was going to be on a higher plane in ancient, honeyed quadrangles dripping with wisteria. On his first day in 1916 the young Bates was twice assaulted by other boys on the train before catching his first glimpse of his new school: 'The school was newly built, of fresh red brick, not at all beautiful, and stood in a large asphalt playground. It was a little grander, but not much, than the school I had left. There were no quadrangles and no vast playing fields of grass with avenues of quiet elms.'

Harrow School and Eton College are widely known to have perfected the mawkish 'school song'. In H. A. Vachell's novel, *The Hill*, even a field marshal with a Victoria Cross wells up during the last verse of 'Forty Years On', the Harrow School song:

> Forty years on, when afar and asunder
> Parted are those who are singing today,
> When you look back, and forgetfully wonder,
> What you were like in your work and your play.
> Then, it may be, there will often come o'er you,
> Glimpses of notes like the catch of a song –
> Visions of boyhood shall float them before you,
> Echoes of dreamland shall bear them along.

While the 'Eton Boating Song' ends in a way guaranteed to make grown men weep freely:

> Twenty years hence this weather
> May tempt us from office stools:
> We may be slow on the feather,
> And seem to the boys old fools:
> But we'll still swing together,
> And swear by the best of Schools.

Winston Churchill had only fond memories of St George's Preparatory School in Ascot, which he left to go to Harrow in 1888:

> Flogging with the birch in accordance with the Eton fashion was a great feature in its curriculum. But I am sure no Eton boy, and certainly no Harrow boy of my day, ever received such a cruel flogging as this Headmaster was accustomed to inflict upon the little boys who were in his care and power . . . Two or three times a month the whole school was marshalled in the Library, and one or more delinquents were hauled off to an adjoining apartment by the two head boys, and there flogged until they bled freely, while the rest sat quaking, listening to their screams . . .

THE LEGENDARY TOP FIVE FLOGGING HEADMASTERS

1. **DR JOHN KEATE** of Eton beat an average of ten boys each day, excluding Sunday. On 30 June 1832, he thrashed over eighty of his pupils at the end of which he received a standing ovation from the school.

2. **DR BUSBY** of Westminster was 'regarded by flagellants as perhaps the finest expert with the rod that England has ever known'.

3. **DR CHARLES VAUGHAN** of Harrow was said to have been unmoved when *The Times* ran a piece on a Harrow monitor who'd given thirty-one strokes of the cane to a lad named Stewart, 'from the effects of which he suffered so severely as to require medical care'.

4. **DR RIDDING** of Winchester College was known to beat fifty boys at a time after morning school.

5. **THE REV. H. W. MOSS** of Shrewsbury School inflicted eighty-eight strokes on a boy who'd smuggled alcohol into his study. 'Mere fleabites,' he called the weals and bruises that were discovered by the surgeon ten days after the beating.

Unparalleled Culinary Delights: British Food and Drink

'I F YOU WANT TO EAT WELL IN ENGLAND,' said Somerset Maugham, 'eat three breakfasts.' Or better still, go straight to the dessert. British food is traditionally cooked in a sealed pot or roasting oven. All the ingredients go in together, and there they stay until they are done. Failing that, a deep-fat frying pan is just as good. As soon as the raw ingredients hit the fat, they are ready to eat. The British don't have the patience to stand over a hob. If a dish is going to take time, then it had better be a steamed pudding with custard.

In 1530, John Roose was convicted of poisoning a pot of broth intended for the family of the Bishop of Rochester. To show his special displeasure, Henry VIII passed a law to have John Roose boiled alive. Execution by

[32]

boiling stayed on the statute books until 1863, but the relationship between English cooking and a slow and painful death lingers on.

> *'English cuisine is generally so threadbare that for years there has been a gentlemen's agreement in the civilized world to allow the Brits pre-eminence in the matter of tea – which, after all, comes down to little more than the ability to boil water.'*
>
> *GQ* magazine, 1984

In the 1960s, British pub-goers still preferred warm draught beers with enticing names like 'Old Speckled Hen' than bottled lager. Market research showed that male British drinkers associated bottled beer with continental Europe. To make it acceptable to them, television advertisers concentrated on the ordinary British diamond geezer in the pub, who would 'stay sharp to the bottom of the glass' by drinking Harp lager, or attract gorgeous women by following the 'Hofmeister Bear'. The anglicization of suave, Continental lager drinking was a complete success. Forty years on, the British 'lager lout' is a singer of drunken songs and a wearer of Union Jack underpants on his head.

A law passed in 1776 required anyone found in possession of a large quantity of 'sloe leaves, or the leaves of ash, elder or any other tree' to prove that the leaves had not been gathered for 'the purpose of fabricating and manufacturing the same in imitation of tea'. The fine was five pounds or up to a year in gaol. Who would ever doubt that tea-drinking is a serious business in Britain?

To keep his subjects fit for fighting the French, Edward III passed the Sumptuary Act of 1336, which prohibited the eating of more than two courses at mealtime. The law specified that soup was a course in its own right and not a sauce. Ploughmen, in particular, were warned to eat moderately. This does not excuse, much less forgive, the ubiquitous 'Ploughman's Lunch' found on modern British pub menus.

In 1642, Cromwell banned mince pies at Christmas, along with plum puddings, Yule logs and decking the halls with holly. He wanted a fast on Christmas Day instead, 'because it may call to remembrance our sins and the sins of our forefathers, who have turned this feast, pretending the memory of Christ, into an extreme forgetfulness of Him by giving liberty to carnal and sensual delights, contrary to the life which Christ Himself led here on earth.' British people are in general agreement that Cromwell's government was right about many things, but in the end much too boring to make a go of it.

Henry VIII set the punishment for anyone that struck a blow and drew blood within the precincts of his palace. The law stayed on the statute books until 1829. Note the culinary flavour to the punishment. In England, there has long been a tradition of kitchen staff doling out torture.

1. And the Master Cook shall deliver a dressing-knife to the Sergeant of the Larder, who shall be then and there ready, and hold upright the dressing-knife till the execution be done.
2. And the Sergeant of the Woodyard shall bring to the said place of execution a block, with cords to bind the said hand upon the block while the execution is in doing.
3. And the Yeomen of the Scullery to prepare and make at the place of execution a fire of coals, and there to make ready searing-irons.

4. And the Groom of the Salcery shall be also then and there ready with vinegar and cold water, and give attendance upon the Surgeon until the same execution be done.

5. And the Sergeant of the Pantry shall be also then and there ready to give bread to the party that shall have his hand so stricken off.

6. And the Sergeant of the Cellar shall also be then and there ready with a pot of red wine to give the same party drink after his hand is so stricken off and the stump seared.

The British must concede that the culinary influence of the French has been a force for good. Even the English national dish owes something to the French, whose idea of chipped potatoes came to England in the middle of the nineteenth century. Until then, the natural accompaniment of cooked fish was bread or baked potato. From 1865, 'fish 'n' chips' became inseparable.

❀

When it comes to the 'vice of drunkenness' the English are world-beaters. They drink more devotedly, more urgently, more copiously, and with much less imagination than the French, Germans and Americans. In drinking terms, 'This blessèd spot, this earth, this realm, this

England, this nurse' of potent hangovers is a centre of excellence. The eighth-century missionary St Boniface saw in the sozzled Englishman a lingering pagan influence unheard of in 'the Franks, nor the Gauls, nor the Lombards, nor the Romans, nor the Greeks . . .' The twelfth-century historian William of Malmesbury blamed the English army's defeat at Hastings on drunkenness ('in which occupation they passed entire nights as well as days').

In 1475, the English King Edward IV removed his army from Calais in exchange for large amounts of French food and wine. 'I have chased the English out of France more easily than my father ever did,' boasted the French King Louis, 'for my father drove them out by force of arms, whereas I have driven them out with venison pies and good wine.' In truth, he needn't have wasted *good* wine on the English.

During the First World War, the British government tackled the problem of drunkenness among munitions workers by limiting the opening hours of pubs, thereby punishing all drinkers. Almost a century on, at eleven o'clock sharp each night, bar staff around the country drop their smiles and start yelling at punters whose company until now they had seemed to enjoy. They ring bells, bang gongs, wrestle away chairs from bottoms and snatch away half-finished drinks. It is this final outrage that has taught generations of Brits to throw back any quantity of alcohol without expectation of enjoyment. It is considered a crime against nature to leave anything but spit in your glass when leaving a British pub. Sadly though, this most unique and traditional approach to drinking may well become a thing of the past, since in 2005 licencees were given the chance to extend their licensing hours to beyond the usual eleven o'clock deadline. Perhaps one day the Brits will find themselves savouring each and every mouthful of wine or beer, in no rush to leave a café or bar, in a fashion akin to their European neighbours . . . Then again, perhaps not.

> *'They are like their own beer; froth on top, dregs at bottom, the middle excellent.'*
>
> VOLTAIRE, on the British

The Regency hellraiser Squire John 'Jack' Mytton is said to have consumed six bottles of port a day. He had a bottle on hand while shaving in the morning, sunk three or four glasses in the afternoon, another bottle with dinner, and several glasses after dinner, and he took a bottle up to bed with him to see him off to sleep. He died aged thirty-seven, after spending the last twelve years of his life in a more or less permanent state of drunkenness.

In the late 1980s, when imported Continental lagers were seriously eroding the sales of traditional British beer, the enterprising microbiologist Dr Keith Thomas tried to re-inject some patriotism into the drinking habits of young men. The wreck of a nineteenth-century sailing barge that was discovered off the Sussex coast yielded fifty bottles of a strong dark ale, popular in the nineteenth century, called porter. It tasted of 'old, wet boots,' said Dr Thomas, but he managed to isolate some live yeast which he used to ferment ingredients taken from an old recipe. The patriotic name of his limited-edition drink, faithfully recreated with authentic nineteenth-century yeast, was Flag Original. Needless to say, imported Continental lagers remain the preferred drink of young men in the twenty-first century.

The British are unable to express open sensual pleasure in drink. Though Britain is the home of wine connoisseurship, wine is an intellectual rather than a sensual stimulant, to be enjoyed through analysis.

After the Norman Conquest, while the dispossessed English tended the sheep, cows and pigs in the fields, the French landowner enjoyed eating the fruits of his labours, the *mouton*, *boeuf* and *porc* at his table. In the fields the animal is English; as soon as it's cooked, it becomes French.

Never confess to an English person that you are a dab hand in the kitchen. If faced with the casual inquiry, 'Anything nice for supper?' the correct response is 'Not really' or 'Something out of the freezer' or, at a push, 'Got some marrow from the garden that wants eating.' Never admit that you own a recipe book or intend to mix ingredients, or it will seem that you are adopting airs.

Love Thy Neighbour:
The French Problem

W HEN WILLIAM THE CONQUEROR DIED IN 1087, he gave his
  eldest son, Robert Curthose, his most important territory,
Normandy. The younger son, William Rufus,
got England. Throughout the Middle Ages,
kings of England were born and educated
in France. They married French
princesses, and when they died, they were
buried – some of them – in French
churches. They *were* French. Even
Henry VIII was conscious of the
cultural inferiority of the
English. He wrote love letters in
French to Anne Boleyn, who
had changed her name from
Bullen to the French-sounding Boleyn through
education and taste. 'Is't possible,' asks the Lord Chamberlain in
Shakespeare's *Henry VIII*, 'the spells of France should juggle Men into such
strange mysteries?'

'Fraid so, Shakey.

After the Norman Conquest, the English did what they have always done in the face of a new, complicated foreign language. They failed to learn it. Instead they loosely adopted around 10,000 French words, without worrying about correct pronunciation, and kept on speaking English. The innate laziness of the English to learn foreign languages ensured the survival of English and its later near-domination of the globe.

Within sixty years of the conquest of 1066, the Normans took over every position of power in church and state. 'No Englishman today is an Earl or Bishop or Abbot,' wrote the historian William of Malmesbury. 'The newcomers gnaw at the wealth and guts of England, nor is there any hope of ending the misery.' A thousand years on, the English prefer to look back on the early Middle Ages in England as an agreeable absorption of the French element. England took what it liked – castles, cathedrals, the Christian names William and Henry – and left the rest.

Top fifteenth-century constitutional lawyer Sir John Fortescue in his treaties *On the Gouvernance of England*, boasted that 'there bith more Men hanged in Englond in a Yere for Robberye and Manslaughter than there be hangid in Fraunce for such manner of crime in seven Yers.' His point was not that the French were more law-abiding than the English, but that the French were not bold enough to commit violent crime like the English. (Fortescue is, of course, a French-derived surname.)

Horatio Nelson once called a midshipman to his cabin to give him the three essentials for surviving in the Royal Navy. First, 'Obey orders.' Second, 'Consider every man as your enemy who speaks ill of your King.' Third, 'Hate a Frenchman as you do the Devil.'

The English King Edward III rode into a French market town one morning, and nailed a proclamation on to the nearest church door announcing that he was actually the rightful King of France. The nettled response of the French King that follows adequately frames the European reaction to what is now widely seen as the birth of the English ego: 'We know for certain that, through inducement and very wicked and false counsel, the King of England, mortal enemy to ourselves and our kingdom, scornfully using the most wicked deceit and malice, has caused to be written many letters, sealed with his seal, in which are contained falsehoods, lies, treason and things injurious to us, to our kingdom and to our subjects . . . '

'How pleasant a sight to see the English so discomfited!' wrote the nephew of the French King Charles VI (reigned 1380–1422), reacting jubilantly to the loss of English lands in France in a letter penned during a twenty-five-year stretch in an English prison. 'Discomfited,' indeed.

In 1558, Queen Mary I lost Calais, England's last toehold in France, but English monarchs continued to style themselves as Kings and Queens of France until 1802, when the Revolution robbed them of a kingdom to covet and brought them war with France again. They later helped to restore the exiled Louis XVIII to the French throne, and resumed hostilities.

[44]

One of a new breed of Tudor warship, equipped with heavy cannon, the *Mary Rose* sank in front of the mocking French fleet when water flooded through her lower gundecks as she turned out to sea from Portsmouth Harbour. Watching from the shore, Henry VIII is said to have screamed like a girl. In 1982, the sodden and sand-filled carcass of the warship-that-never-went-to-war was raised from the seabed to patriotic fanfares after a high-profile, four-month recovery operation. In Britain, a monumental disaster is worth a thousand small victories.

A great number of English baby boys are named after the French bigwigs who conquered England in 1066. The most popular first names recall Kings William, Henry, Richard, Stephen, and John, while names like Guy, Hugh, and Simon pay homage to sundry Norman knights. Children saddled with good old-fashioned, pre-Conquest, Saxon names like Wulfric, Wulfstan, Egbert, Dunstan, Aelfric or Ethelbert are mocked without mercy and quickly revert to their less amusing Anglo-Norman middle names. You meet few Edgars and Herewards nowadays, and as for Cnut (actually a Viking name), any chance of a revival was probably doomed when French Connection launched its 'FCUK' promotion . . .

How the English should have pronounced the post-Conquest kings of England, had they had any aptitude for foreign languages:

Guillaume I le Conquérant (1066–87)
Guillaume II (1087–1100)
Henri I (1100–35)
Étienne de Blois (1135–54)
Henri II Courtmanteau (1154–89)
Richard I Coeur de Lion (1189–99)
Jean Sans Terre (1199–1216)
Henri III (1216–72)
Édouard I (1272–1307)
Édouard II (1307–27)
Édouard III (1327–77)
Richard II (1377–99)
Henri IV (1399–1413)

'The day after [King Stephen's] arrival, he drew up his army containing a great number of excellent and distinguished knights . . . the floodgates of Heaven opened, and such bitter gusts of wind and pouring rain were driven into their faces, that God himself seemed to be fighting for the Duke [of Aquitaine] . . . He and his men had the gale at their backs; the King's men had it in their faces, so that they could barely hold their weapons or their dripping lances . . .'

This 'duke' of Aquitaine, who clearly had the best of the weather on this occasion, was later crowned Henry II. The King of England may have been French, but according to the twelfth-century English chronicler Henry of Huntingdon in his *Historia Anglorum – The History of the English People* (1135), it was the English weather that chose him.

> *'Come now, you village folk*
> *Who love the French king,*
> *Be of good cheer, all of you,*
> *In our fight against the English.*
> *Each of you take a hoe*
> *And you'll find it easier to uproot them.*
> *If you find they're staying put*
> *Then at least pull faces at them.*
> *Don't be afraid.*
> *Go and fight those Goddams,*
> *Beer-guts every one of them,*
> *Because every single one of us*
> *Is worth four of them*
> *Well, three of them anyway . . .'*

An old French drinking song
exhorting the French peasantry
to kick the English out of France

During the Hundred Years War between England and France (which actually took place over a 116-year period, from 1337 until 1453), *godon* was the French slang for an English soldier. Today, an Englishman abroad for any other reason than to lie belly-up on a hot beach has everything in common with the disgruntled medieval campaigner whose defining phrase is *God damn!*

Concern for the moral character of the traditional enemy has wormed its way into the English *and* French languages. In France, *un tor de Englois* is a crafty throw in wrestling, while Dr Johnson's English dictionary defines *ruse* as 'cunning; artifice; little stratagem; trick; wile; fraud; deceit – a French word neither elegant nor necessary.'

> *'England? Fine soil,
> but bad people.'*
>
> French proverb

'When I am dead and my body is opened,' Queen Mary is supposed to have said without flinching at the thought, 'ye shall find CALAIS written on my heart.' Of all the hideous concrete and diesel-soaked booze-cruise destinations to make the subject of a final romantic tattooing gesture, her choice of Calais must be one she now regrets.

The passenger-carrying hot-air balloon, the parachute jump, the metric system, the diver's helmet with respirator, the buoyancy life-vest, the breech-loading cannon, the rapid-fire rifle, the screw tourniquet, and the use of forceps are things that the British would like to have invented, but the French got there first.

Parts of the English language are minted in a Francophobic gutter: 'French tricks' is a euphemism for oral sex; 'French prints' are pornographic pictures; condoms are known as 'French letters'; syphilis went by the name 'French gout', and the quaint phrase 'a blow from a French faggot-stick' meant to lose one's nose through syphilis. Interestingly, the fact that the word 'French' is synonymous with sex in the English language, and the French phrase for a condom is *une capote anglaise,* seems to imply that the French think the same of the English, which suggests that people, whatever their nationality, think that foreigners always get more sex.

Brits in Battle: Invasions, Rebellions, Riots and Other General Mayhem

BATTLES, MASSACRES, INSURRECTIONS, REBELLIONS, UPRISINGS, call them what you like, the British love a good scrap. There is no cause or belief so pure and noble that it can't be reduced by the British into an ugly street fight. There have been riots against turnpike roads, land enclosures, newfangled agricultural and printing machines, taxes, immigrant communities and coalpit closures. Rioters hope that the authorities will respond with disproportionate force to justify their violent backlash, and another few days of mayhem. The authorities usually oblige. 'In England,' writes Jeremy Paxman, 'street insurrection is less often to do with politics and more to do with innate readiness to trade punches.'

The Monmouth Rebellion of 1685 is remembered fondly as the 'last popular rebellion' in English history culminating in the 'last battle' on English soil. So thoroughly have its events been washed in an end-of-era glow that to think about Monmouth is to miss those carefree days when it was possible to land a few ships at Lyme Regis, raise an army of scythe-wielding peasants in the West Country, march on London and still have change from a pound.

On 5 November each year, British people let off fireworks in fields and squeeze their children affectionately while watching an effigy of a man called Guy Fawkes (usually just a couple of binliners stuffed with paper, wearing jumble-sale clothes and sporting a leftover Halloween mask) burst into flames on the nearby bonfire. During the evening, perhaps, some folk try to recall the events of the 1605 Gunpowder Plot, in which a group of

English Catholic radicals tried to kill King James I of England and the Protestant nobility by blowing up the Houses of Parliament during the State Opening of Parliament; in stark contrast, however, the majority are content to endure cricked necks as they stare up into the night sky and whoop with delight at the pretty colours, and the heart-stopping sounds of the fireworks whizzing through the air.

Like so much British pageantry, the cosy event wears a dark and barbarous undertone. The English, extraordinary though it sounds, were not so long ago a nation of religious zealots, straining to lynch another Catholic plotter and sniffing out Catholic priests in their hiding places. 'I never yet knew a treason without a Catholic priest,' said the chief prosecutor at the trial of the Gunpowder Plotters. The bonfire festivities were a time for concerted Catholic-baiting, until the Riot Act was read to the most raucous of them in the nineteenth century. Only St Peter's School in York has never celebrated Guy Fawkes Night, it being considered rather bad form to engage in the ritualistic burning of an effigy of an Old Boy.

In spite of the exciting-sounding name, the 'Glorious Revolution' of 1688 was neither glorious nor revolutionary. The de-throning of (Catholic) King James II by (Protestant) William of Orange has all the hallmarks of invasion by committee: a pasty-faced, decidedly unheroic Dutchman, a tedious slogan ('for the Protestant religion and the liberties of England') and an absence of a good fight at the end. To this day – in spite of those big and stimulating words – it's unlikely that any English father has ever sat down his son and told him the tale of the Glorious Revolution.

In 1497 Michael an Gof led a Cornish army of 15,000 men to London to pick a fight with Henry VIII who had raised Cornish taxes one time too many. An Gof's peasant rabble was met on Blackheath, on the southeastern outskirts of London, by the entire English army about to march off to the Scottish wars. It is uncertain whether an Gof died on the gallows at Tyburn dreaming of a 'fame permanent and immortal', as the Cornish maintain, or if he was kicking himself for not holding off the revolt until the English army was away in Scotland. In all the excitement he obviously forgot the crucial maxim used by rebels the world over – timing is everything.

Popular British disdain for intellectuals finds a distant but true echo in an Oxford riot in 1355. It began as a brawl between locals and students in the city-centre Swyndlestock Tavern and developed into an all-out street fight. The tolling bell summoned the townsfolk in from the fields who shouted, 'Havac! Havac! Smyt fast, give gode knocks!' They stormed the students' hostels, scalped a number of chaplains, jumped a procession of friars and murdered sixty-three scholars. To this day it remains the case that 'townies' frighten the pants off students – an early indication of the age-old rivalry between 'Town' and 'Gown'.

To British class warriors, the Battle of Kinder Scout of 1932 is comparable
to nothing less than General Wolfe's night-time assault on Quebec in 1757.
In this case, the raiding party consisted of ramblers from Manchester and
Sheffield, and their assault of the Peak District's highest privately owned
upland, in the cause of the 'right to roam', met doughty resistance from a
posse of be-tweeded, shotgun-wielding gamekeepers. Grapplings in the
peat bog startled the grouse. The ringleaders of the rambling troops were
flung in prison on charges of riotous assembly, but the day was theirs.

The Peterloo Massacre of 1819 took place on fields just outside Manchester. Around 50,000 people had gathered to listen to radical orator Henry Hunt calling for an extension of the vote to all adults. In an attempt to arrest Hunt, the local yeomanry (part-time cavalrymen) arrived on horseback with their sabres in the air, leaving eleven dead and another six hundred wounded. After Peterloo, politicians feared revolution in Britain. To this day, the working class has regretted an opportunity missed.

The Romantic History of Britain favours gallant dreamers, charismatic fools and noble underdogs above stern and impregnable kings. Its heroes must at all costs look good on a horse and possess a stock of personal charm. The odds must be stacked against him. Too much planning looks bad; he must possess the unworldly character of a doomed hero. In the end he must die on the battlefield in a desperate last charge, disappear into European obscurity on a fishing boat, or face hideous public execution with composure, quipping with the axeman. Bonnie Prince Charlie, William Wallace, and the Duke of Monmouth are examples, but doubt lingers over precisely how good the Cornish patriot Michael an Gof looked on a horse. (Probably, he couldn't afford one.)

Eccentrics: Great British 'Characters'

S OME SLIGHT DEGREE OF MADNESS is seen as welcome and desirable in British people. If they don't have it, they fake it. 'I'm mad, me!' shouts the fat-larry in the rampaging shopping trolley who is really old enough to know better. And the pimply-faced office new boy simply must expect to meet a dreary old-timer balancing a paperweight on his head who insists, 'You don't have to be mad to work here, but it helps!' The fact is that even vaguely sensible-looking people around Britain openly collect things like traffic cones (of which there are somewhere in the range of 530 variations), corkscrews, cinema organs, lawn mowers, milk bottles, airsick bags, nutcrackers, and fishing buoys. In most cases, however, British collectors engage in such practices as a means of quietly avoiding other human beings who are as awkward and peculiar as themselves.

THE GOURMET: The nineteenth-century Oxford professor Dean William Buckland claimed to have eaten his way through half the animal kingdom, proclaiming with authority that mole tasted the worst, while the common housefly was not much better. In his rooms in Christ Church College, where guests would often be offered battered mice at breakfast, he even kept a hyena, which leads one to wonder whether the poor animal was fated to end up on the deranged professor's plate as so many other creatures before it.

He once denounced a miracle in an Italian church by licking the darkened spot on the flagstones said to be the fresh blood of a martyr, announcing that it was bat urine. Stranded in his carriage in a night-time fog west of London, he scooped some earth from the road, tasted it, and declared to his companions, 'Gentlemen, Uxbridge!'

Perhaps the worst example of his most baffling behaviour occurred after supper one evening at the Harcourt estate in Oxfordshire. It was during this gathering that a strange-looking morsel was handed around the table, each guest politely passing it on. According to his custom, Buckland popped it straight into his mouth and swallowed it down. The incredulous look on his host's face screamed *faux pas*; for the mysterious object was the pickled heart of the Sun King, Louis XIV of France, a prized Harcourt heirloom.

THE INCURABLE NOSTALGIC: Charles Paget Wade suffered a particular type of English obsession for 'bygones', though the evils of private wealth and an excess of leisure-time drove his mania to an advanced stage. His collection of Indonesian masks, model boats, Civil War weapons, spinning wheels, penny farthings and Japanese armour – never single pieces, always dozens of them – gradually overwhelmed every room of his Cotswolds home, forcing Wade into an outhouse, which gradually filled up too.

A man governed by whims, Wade (who died in 1956) chose his gardener based on his name – which was Hodge – and his hat – 'which was mauve' – and the fact that he knew nothing about gardening beyond cabbages and cauliflowers. In Wade's addled opinion, therefore, 'Here was the very man.'

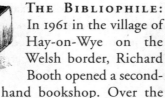

THE BIBLIOPHILE: In 1961 in the village of Hay-on-Wye on the Welsh border, Richard Booth opened a second-hand bookshop. Over the next sixteen years, he opened more bookshops and settled rather too naturally into the role of eccentric book-fancier. On 1 April 1977, in front of a small assembly of loyal friends and local journalists, wearing a copper crown and holding a plumber's ballcock, Booth crowned himself King of Hay, which he declared was an independent country, and achieved worldwide publicity.

THE DREAMER: Beware an idealistic Englishman with a nostalgic turn of mind and a plan, because before you know it, you will be waking up at dawn to feed poultry and living off radish soup, while attempting to earn a living by fashioning jewellery out of driftwood.

In 1902, Charles Robert Ashby of the London Guild and School of Handicraft convinced dozens of sensible East End craftsmen to move to the village of Chipping Campden in Gloucestershire. Intimidating the locals apparently wasn't Ashby's only aim in bringing cockneys to the Cotswolds, although in this he can claim a great success. He set them to work making jewellery and metalwork, and organized dances and ran cookery classes. When the venture failed after four years, Ashby's Cotswold craftsmen returned to London, where it is said, they never did touch another cream tea.

THE BULL-NECKED RADICAL: The author of *Rural Rides* (1830), William Cobbett failed in a big way. He failed at everything he did, and took failing to new heights. Dogged, bone-headed resilience was a kind of art form with him. In 1782, at the age of nineteen, he tried to join the Navy but failed. Two years later he joined the Army, but had to flee the country after rashly accusing officers of embezzlement. He ended up in America, where he set himself up as a bookseller, and wrote a string of prickly anti-republican articles. He was fined $5,000 for accusing a doctor of killing his patients.

Back in England, meanwhile, his own newspaper the *Porcupine's Gazette* folded. An article against flogging, which was published in his weekly radical journal, the *Political Register*, landed him in court for sedition. He defended himself, lost, and was sent to Newgate Prison, emerging two years later to stand as parliamentary candidate for Southampton. He lost and was offered £10,000 by the government to retire from politics and stop publishing his *Political Register*. He refused, campaigned as the Member of Parliament for Coventry in 1820, lost, filed for bankruptcy, and lost two pending libel actions with costs and damages against him. At last, aged seventy and at his fifth attempt, in 1832 he got into the House of Commons as MP for Oldham, Lancashire, and spent the rest of his life making inflammatory speeches.

> *'George the Third,*
> *Ought never to have occurred;*
> *Such an absurd accident,*
> *Is entirely without precedent.'*
>
> A subversive verse attributed
> to WILLIAM COBBETT

THE HELLRAISER: Heir to a private fortune of £60,000 and an annual income of £10,000 due on his twenty-first birthday in 1817, John 'Jack' Mytton cheerfully messed up careers in the Seventh Hussars and the

House of Commons before concentrating his efforts on his talent for mayhem. There was nothing Jack wouldn't attempt for a bet, including hunting in the nude and riding a two-horse carriage cross-country at night through hedges and ditches. He was a gambler, drinker and brawler, once going at least twelve bare-knuckle rounds with a Welsh miner before the other man surrendered. He rode into dinner on a bear on one memorable occasion, and later robbed his own guests dressed as a highwayman. Forced to flee his creditors, he ended up in Calais in 1830, where, in an attempt to frighten away an attack of hiccups, he set fire to his shirt. Returning to England two years' later, he endured an alcoholic's demise in King's Bench debtors' prison in London, where he died aged thirty-seven.

Foreigners' Fun: Making Fools of the British

Τ HE BRITISH PRIDE THEMSELVES on their common sense. They see it as one of their God-given endowments. It is one of the many perks, as it were, of being British. How unlucky to be foreign, and saddled with things that make no sense, like a hot temper, superstitions, passion, and the need for afternoon naps. Good sense, like a good cup of tea, is the property of the British.

In 1770, the great British explorer James Cook set out in search of a legendary continent in the southern seas. His expedition arrived at Port Jackson, now Sydney Harbour, and asked the name of the peculiar creature hopping around like a giant rabbit: 'I don't understand what you're asking,' said the Aboriginal in his own language; a surprisingly short sentence that roughly translates as 'Kangaroo'.

In the eighteenth century, the South Sea Company won exclusive rights to trade with Spanish America and the Pacific. Things went well, trade boomed. They hiked the value of their stock. Shares went up, fortunes were made. Then it dawned on shareholders that to pay the dividend would require an impossible profit. The bubble burst, thousands faced ruin. The Sub-Governor of the company, Sir John Fellowes, was stripped of his estates and a fortune of £300,000 (about £3 million in today's money). The Governor got off because he was King George I.

The British royal family is of almost unblemished German descent. The House of Hanover put four Georges and one William on the throne. Queen Victoria was born in Germany, married to a German (Albrecht von Sachsen-Coburg und Gotha, or Prince Albert), and spoke German to her German relatives. Yet she was groomed to look and sound in speech and manners like the soul of the British Empire, that soul being *southern* English (and mannered and moneyed southern English, at that). After the outbreak of war with Germany in 1914, the German connection needed to be downplayed. George V distanced himself from his German cousin, Kaiser Wilhelm II, by changing his name from Sachsen-Coburg (or Saxe-Coburg) und Gotha to Windsor. The House of Windsor maintains its foreign credentials in the present queen's marriage to Philip von Schleswig-Holstein-Sonderburg-Glücksburg, Prince of Greece and Denmark. Similarly, the Duke of Edinburgh's uncle, Prince Louis of Battenberg, assumed the surname Mountbatten in July 1917, with the result that minor royals are now surnamed Mountbatten-Windsor.

As a schoolboy, Thomas Chatterton, the son of a Bristol schoolmaster, had a precocious talent for pseudo-medieval poetry. In 1767, when he found fragments of antique blank parchment in a forgotten chest at St Mary Redcliffe Church, Bristol, he started passing off his work as that of a fictitious fifteenth-century monk, 'Thomas Rowley'. Soon literary tongues of London were wagging about this hitherto unknown genius. Once the fraud was discovered, the only comfort for those within the literati who had been made to look foolish by the teenager-poet was Chatterton's eventual public exposure, destitution and ultimate suicide, aged seventeen.

In July 1802, a holidaying gentleman calling himself the Hon. Alexander Augustus Hope impressed the local gentry of Keswick in the Lake District by dropping hints of his noble connections and enormous wealth. He took his splendid carriage to the village of Buttermere, where he fell in love with the local landowner's daughter, a famous local beauty called Mary Robinson. They married in October, and honeymooned around the Lake District. Then the police arrived and it was revealed that the so-called nobleman was neither heir to a huge personal fortune, nor in the least bit honourable, but rather a failed commercial traveller named John Hatfield with abandoned wives all around England. He was hanged in Carlisle on 3 September 1803, but not for bigamy, as you would think, but for defrauding the Post Office by franking his own letters without permission, which was a capital offence in those days. After the fuss had died down, the Lakes author Thomas de Quincey quietly travelled to Buttermere to see the famous beauty for himself, and noted 'She was none of your evanescent, wasp-waisted beauties . . . Everything about her face and bust was negative, simply without offence . . . but she was what all the world would have agreed to call "good looking".'

The Royal Society was the most august gentleman's club of the seventeenth century. Its founding members included chemist Robert Boyle, diarist John Evelyn and architect Christopher Wren. However, not all of its sessions achieved the appropriate blend of earnest inquiry plus good, common sense. In January 1663, the antiquarian John Aubrey was made a Fellow, and on the day of his admission, he presented to the Society 'the scheme of a cart with legs instead of wheels'. What sort of a notion was that? Oh, to have seen the bemused faces of his fellow Fellows.

How the British would like to believe in fairies, those mischievous little people dressed in all their finery at the bottom of the garden. Mostly, they content themselves with having garden gnomes, but in 1916 in Cottingley, near Bradford, two little girls, Elsie Wright and her cousin Frances Griffiths, made believers out of sensible grown-ups by claiming to have photographed a group of fairies mid-flight using Elsie's camera. Word reached Sir Arthur Conan Doyle (creator of Sherlock Holmes and a firm believer in the paranormal), who even asked the girls for more fairy pictures. They obliged four years later. Only in 1972, when Elsie sold her camera to buy an electric lawnmower, did she admit the fairies were cut-outs, rigged up for photography using hatpins and knicker elastic.

In the eighteenth century, medicine was in the hands of unregulated quack doctors. Treatments routinely included ground insects, rhubarb in any form, and a course of leeches. Roasted onion helped with ear trouble and the tail of a black tomcat warded off eye infections, though it is not clear whether the tom's tail was to be sucked, swallowed or merely stroked. A swig of gin and a quick dip in the village pond cured the ague. The remedy for 'Whirligigousticon' is mercifully unrecorded.

In the Stratford-upon-Avon area, no fewer than five houses charge visitors an entrance fee based on claims of being connected in some way to William Shakespeare. In November 2000, 'Mary Arden's House' at Wilmcote in Aston Cantlow – a timber-framed farmhouse in which it was believed that Mary, Shakespeare's mother, had lived prior to her marriage to John Shakespeare – was found to have been incorrectly named. An obscure document had been discovered, proving that the alleged 'Mary Arden's House' had not even been built until five years after Mary had left the village. For seventy years, millions of visitors had been wasting their reverential hush on a house that had absolutely nothing to do with William Shakespeare. Strangely, no one seemed to mind in the slightest. The real 'Mary Arden's House' can be found at Glebe Farm, a mere stone's throw from the erroneously titled Wilmcote address, now called Palmer's Farm.

Sex and the Brits

I<small>N</small> B<small>RITAIN</small>, <small>SEX MUST BE IMPLIED WITH A WINK</small>, a flash of thigh, an air-brushed bosom, a crude innuendo, but never openly declared. The British have never got used to the idea of people having sex with each other. Sex is something that they personally do, and one or two people they know do, that footballers do a lot, and public servants do only for the purpose of producing future taxpayers – if it turns out that public servants have done it for any other reason, if the British people are forced to look at photographic evidence of the fact in newspapers they normally avoid, then it's called a great British scandal.

In the 1890s, the well-known Cambridge prostitute Daisy Hopkins was arrested by university constables and charged by the Vice-Chancellor's Court with 'walking with a member of the university in a public street of the town of Cambridge and within the precincts of the university'. 'Walking' was the university's euphemism for selling sex.

She was given fourteen days in the spinning house. But Daisy appealed on the grounds that 'walking' was not a crime. The Chief Justice agreed with Daisy, and overturned her sentence: 'Nobody would suppose that a person simply walking with a member of the university, who might be that member's mother, or sister, or wife, or friend, was guilty of an offence against the law which would justify the Vice-Chancellor in imprisoning him or her.' Quite so. British law has always had trouble with the business of framing laws on prostitution, which does, of course, involve admitting to its very existence. Today, the world's oldest service industry can go about its business, so long as it doesn't advertise its wares on the streets. So not much has changed then . . .

Henry VIII passed one of his trademark catch-all laws in 1536, but the final clause carries the weight of it: 'An Act for the Continue of the Statutes for Beggars and Vagabonds; and against Conveyance of Horses and Mares out of this Realm; against Welshmen making Affrays in the Counties of Hereford, Gloucester and Salop; and against the vice of Buggery.'

In 1351, Edward III showed himself to be a normal red-blooded male by extending the Treason Act to anyone who 'do violate the king's companion, or the king's eldest daughter unmarried, or the wife of the king's eldest son'. Presumably that meant that you could go ahead and violate the king's *youngest* unmarried daughter or the wife of the king's *youngest* son without losing your entrails? Strangely, though, 'Spilling the King's Pint' was left off the statute books.

> **'We are tainted with flagellomania from our childhood.'**
>
> A former Etonian blames frequent schoolboy floggings for his upper-class obsession with bottom spanking, known to the French as *le vice anglais*

The fine for checking into a London hotel under an assumed name for the purpose of shagging is £20. It is also illegal to have sex in trains, buses, parked cars, churchyards, and public parks. Unless all these are managed on the same night, in which case such activity deserves some kind of medal.

William John Bankes of Kingston Lacy in Dorset was an intrepid mid-nineteenth-century traveller and Egyptologist. His excavations of tombs and drawings of rock-cut temples earned the admiration of his peers. When he returned to England, he was caught with a Guardsman sharing a cubicle in a public convenience near Westminster Abbey. The Duke of Wellington testified to his solid, manly character. Ten years later he was caught with another Guardsman on a bench in Green Park. Branded in *The Times* 'a person of wicked, lewd, filthy and unnatural mind', Bankes disappeared to Italy and spent the rest of his days contemplating obelisks (and possibly the insides of Italian public lavatories with local carabinieri, unless his tastes had changed . . .).

In Worthynbury in Flintshire in the Middle Ages, a woman seduced and abandoned by her lover could expect a form of compensation uniquely (and suggestively) appropriate to her situation. A young, well-greased bull was pushed backwards through a wicker door. Two men then goaded it. If she could hold onto the slippery tail, the bull was hers for keeps. Otherwise, she got nothing but a few greasy strands of hair from the bull's tail.

> *'It assumed a horrible, loathsome and often fatal form which in time, as years pass on, the sufferer finds his hair falling off, his skin and the flesh of his body rot, and are eaten away by slow, cankerous and stinking ulcerations; his nose first falls in at the bridge and then rots and falls off; his sight gradually fails and he eventually becomes blind; his voice, first becomes husky and then fades to a hoarse whisper as his throat is eaten away by fetid ulcerations which cause his breath to stink.'*

FIELD MARSHAL LORD KITCHENER puts the fear of something much worse than God into Britain's colonial forces in his 1905 *Memorandum on Syphilis*, in an attempt to warn his troops of the dangers of sowing their wild oats in contaminated ground

The present Marquess of Bath openly maintains a set of 'wifelets' and has painted the walls of Longleat, his stately home in Wiltshire, with lurid sexual murals. The tabloid press christened the virile peer 'Loins of Longleat' after the, erm, lions that made the place famous. His favourite dish is squirrel in mushroom sauce.

The Irish nationalist Sir Roger Casement was arrested in April 1916 soon after landing in Tralee Bay in a German U-boat. As Britain was at war with Germany at the time, he was convicted for treason and the death sentence was passed. Forty senior British politicians and the American government petitioned the Prime Minister, Herbert Asquith, for Casement's reprieve because his actions were politically motivated. When excerpts from Casement's diary showed – in very graphic detail – that he was a raving homosexual, the pressure mysteriously evaporated. The execution went ahead without any fuss.

Two days before the 438th anniversary of William Shakespeare's birthday, a portrait turned up at Hatchlands Park in Surrey of the 'fair youth' to whom Shakespeare's early sonnets are addressed. The portrait shows Shakespeare's patron, Henry Wriothesley, third Earl of Southampton, wearing lipstick, rouge, and double earrings, his long hair hanging down in feminine tresses and his hand on his heart in a camp gesture.

The picture has been authenticated by experts to the precise date when Shakespeare was living in the Southampton household and making the final changes to his new love story, *Romeo and Julian*.

Alexander Keiller was seen as the epitome of the gifted British upper-class amateur for his purchase and excavation of Avebury Henge in the 1930s, and his love of fast cars and skiing. Behind drawn curtains in Berkeley Square he once invited the novelist Antonia White to climb into a laundry basket wearing nothing but a mackintosh so that he could poke her through the wickerwork with an umbrella. 'I have, at different times in my life, made studies, more or less cursory and sometimes merely superficial, of various branches of the erotic impulse,' he casually wrote in his memoirs. Rich people 'make studies', it would seem, while poor people just shag.

A law passed by George I warned that the 'severest Penaltys will be suffered by any commoner who doth permit his animal to have carnal knowledge of a pet of the Royal House'. A case of 'Keep that mongrel away from my corgis,' perhaps?

An obscenity action in Britain forced James Joyce to publish *Ulysses* in Paris. As well as making reference to the f-word and c-word, the 'Big Dirty Book' also features the first ever description of a fictional person sitting on the lavatory 'surrounded by his rising smell'. Joyce's reputation as a randy roger was confirmed in a dirty letter that appeared at auction. Written to his girlfriend Nora Barnacle (his 'strange-eyed whore' whom he later married) during a trip, he describes the many and wonderful ways in which he plans to satisfy his 'ungovernable lust' on his return. 'Heaven forgive my madness,' he signs off.

In *Othello*, Shakespeare puts some memorably lewd phrases into Iago's mouth when Brabantio is informed, 'Your daughter and the Moor are making the beast with the two backs,' and equally vividly, 'an old black Ram is tupping your white Ewe.' These sentences were both mysteriously edited out of Thomas Bowdler's *Family Edition of Shakespeare* in 1818, presumably to avoid the asking of such awkward questions as 'Father, what's "the beast with two backs"?'

[78]

The former Conservative Member of Parliament for Putney, David Mellor, was dubbed 'Minister for Fun' by the media after the tabloid press printed details about an extra-marital affair he had been conducting with an actress, in which it was alleged that during their liaisons his preferred choice of attire was the full Chelsea football kit. Interestingly, the fact of his marital infidelity caused less concern at the time than his choice of football strip.

 In Britain, it has never been illegal to be a homosexual, only to participate in homosexual acts. Lesbianism, on the other hand, is not recognized by law because Queen Victoria refused to acknowledge its existence.

To stop British soldiers forming permanent attachments to local women in the colonies, a steady supply of prostitutes was available wherever soldiers were stationed. A notorious Memorandum of 4 June 1888, which was read out in the House of Commons, rather cheekily called for the provision of 'prettier women' for the troops.

Death and the Brits

NOTHING IMPRESSES THE BRITISH SO MUCH as the grizzly death of a foolhardy explorer in a remote part of the world. Horrible death in the line of duty puts the cherry on the cake of a heroic reputation. Captain James Cook (boiled by the natives of Tahiti), Captain Robert Scott (frozen to death at the South Pole), and Admiral Nelson (pickled in a barrel of brandy, though admittedly shot and killed first) have all benefited posthumously by their manner of perishing. If an heroic death is unavailable, the next best thing is an eccentric burial: vertically in full evening dress being the preferred choice of many a British, upper-class eccentric.

According to his last wishes, famous East Sussex eccentric 'Mad Jack' Fuller was entombed in a pyramid he built for the purpose in Brightling churchyard. He died in 1835, and village lore has it that his 22-stone corpse sits in an iron chair with a bottle of port and a roast chicken before him, waiting for the Resurrection.

Having given away the bearings of his intended final resting place on top of the Lake District mountain of Haystacks in the Buttermere Valley, it occurred to Alfred Wainwright, author of the *Pictorial Guides to the Lakeland Fells,* that his devoted readers might inadvertently bring him back down again in the tread of their hiking boots. He adds in his guide to the Western Fells, 'And if you, dear reader, should get a bit of grit in your boots as you are crossing Haystacks in the years to come, please treat it with respect. It might be me.' Wainwright died in 1991 after a lifetime of walking, drawing and writing.

Yorkshire's 'national' anthem 'On Ilkla' Moor Baht 'At' is the rousing tale of the cannibalism likely to be suffered by a Yorkshireman, written by the West Riding Chapel Choir during a day's ramble on Ilkley Moor, in West Yorkshire. The words are a warning to one of their party who wandered away hatless ('baht' means 'without') from the picnic to smooch with his girlfriend in the heather. The gist is that having forgotten his hat he'll die of cold, and be eaten by worms, the worms will be eaten by ducks, which will be eaten by the Methodist choir group: 'Then we shall all 'av etten thee, On Ilkla' Moor baht'at . . .'

The philosopher Jeremy Bentham left specific and rather laborious instructions for his body after his death: 'My executor will cause the skeleton to be clad in one of the suits of black occasionally worn by me. The body so clothed together with the chair and staff in my later years bourne by me . . .' Since his death in 1832, Bentham's embalmed body sits in state inside a glass case in University College, London, where it can be seen to this day. His head had to be replaced with a replica after students played football with the real thing.

On 3 September 1658, on the night of one of the seventeenth century's greatest storms, Lord Protector Oliver Cromwell died from malaria. His

death was met with some indifference, according to the diarist Ralph Josselin, who revealed 'people not much minding it'. After the Restoration of Charles II on 30 January 1661 (twelve years to the day since Charles I's execution), Cromwell's body was dug up from Westminster Abbey and ceremonially executed. What was left of his head was impaled on a spike at Westminster Hall until it fell off in the wind in 1685. His later burial in an unmarked grave in the grounds of his Alma Mater, Sidney Sussex College, Cambridge, ensures against further molestation.

In the churchyard of St Mary Magdalene in suburban Mortlake is a full-scale stone representation of an Arab sheikh's tent, complete with carved folds frozen, mid-flap, in the breath of a desert breeze. A window in the tent's roof, reached by a steel ladder, reveals the coffins of the nineteenth-century explorer Sir Richard Burton and his wife Isabella.

Rupert Brooke's famous poem 'The Soldier' ('If I should die, think only this of me . . .') was written at the end of 1914, after the poet had volunteered for service with the Royal Navy, at which time he had only a very brief experience of active service in the abortive Antwerp expedition. Brooke was robbed of a soldier's death in action when he suffered a fatal attack of blood poisoning en route to the Dardanelles in 1915.

The pirate Captain Kidd was hanged at Execution Dock in Wapping on 23 May 1701. On the first attempt, the rope broke. Kidd was strung up again, and died quickly. His body was cut down, laid on the  beach and left for the tide to wash over it three times. Then it was painted in tar, bound in chains, and put in a metal harness that would keep his skeleton intact while his flesh rotted. Finally, he was hung from a gibbet at Tilbury Point as a warning to sailors coming in and out of the Thames. On dark nights, the ghost of Captain Kidd has been seen by sailors, apparently (and reasonably, under the circumstances) looking really pissed off.

Thou who passest in silence
Hereby where this body reposeth
Listen to what I shall tell thee
As I am able to tell it.
Such as thou art I have been,
Such as I am thou shalt be:
I thought not at all upon death
While I had vigour and life:
Great riches on earth I possessed
Wherewith great state I maintained;
Lands, horses, and silver and gold;
But now I am poor and depressed,
Deep down in the earth I do lie;
All gone are my beauty and grace,
All wasted away is my flesh,
Very straight and narrow is my abode,
In me there is nothing but truth . . .

EDWARD THE BLACK PRINCE's feel-good epitaph in Canterbury Cathedral

Railway-disaster doggerel was an obscure but vigorous nineteenth-century literary genre, not least because in those days train wrecks were comparatively common, and often costly in casualties. One of its finest expressions – both moving and informative – is the inscription on the tombstone of Thomas Port at St Mary's Church, Harrow-on-the-Hill, London. Port lost both legs and shortly afterwards his life after a tragic train-surfing accident in 1838. So reads his inscription:

> Bright rose the morn and vig'rous Port,
> Gay on the train he used his wonted sport
> 'Ere noon arrived his mangled form they bore
> With pain distorted and overwhelmed with gore
> When evening came to close the fateful day
> A mutilated corpse the sufferer lay . . .

If reading such a delightful account of misadventure isn't enough to put off young hooligans from messing about on railway tracks in modern-day Britain, then God help them.

Gross British Culture

T HE CONVIVIAL BUZZ OF YOUNG AND OLD, artisan and business-
man, talking animatedly in pavement cafés; pétanque played on
gravel plots by elderly men in shirtsleeves; local theatres, galleries and art
centres packed out with families whose pursuit of culture is second only to
their enthusiasm for sitting down together at mealtimes: Britain doesn't do these things. The weather is only partly to blame.

Britain has neatly divided its cultural world in half. Everything on television is considered 'low culture', unless it's a drama by Dennis Potter or cultural commentary presented by Mark Lawson or Melvyn Bragg. All *straight* theatre is 'high culture', unless it features the sound of a gunshot within the first ten minutes, which invariably lowers the tone. Opera and any form

of dance also count as high culture. Musical theatre is irredeemably low. Ironically, even Shakespeare would have been considered low culture in his own day; his London theatre stood outside the city walls among all the other illicit entertainments.

'They love the lever, the screw, the pulley, the Flanders draught-horse, the waterfall, wind-mills, tide-mills; the sea and the wind to bear their freight ships,' wrote Ralph Waldo Emerson of the English, suggesting that ideas instinctively made them nervous. It is perhaps worth noting here that Emerson was American.

> *'The English may not like music
> but they absolutely love the noise it makes.'*
>
> SIR THOMAS BEECHAM, 1944

The 'Protestant Work Ethic' keeps the British hard at work when sensible nations are taking a nap. The PWE comes from the idea that hard work is punishment for the hedonism of Adam and Eve in the Garden of Eden. Unless they are working really hard, the British feel guilty. Combined with their binge-drinking, greasy food and awful sex lives, the stress threatens to make good Oscar Wilde's assessment of 'a typical Englishman, always dull and usually violent.'

> *'This land is blessed with a powerful mediocrity of mind. It has saved you from communism and it has saved you from fascism. In the end, you don't care enough about ideas to suffer their consequences . . . If the Lord God came to England and started expounding His beliefs, you know what they'd say? They'd say, "Oh, come off it!"'*
>
> The Cambridge philosopher GEORGE STEINER
> explains his theory of English pragmatism
> to journalist JEREMY PAXMAN

Sailors brought Britain's most irresistible swearwords back from the Netherlands in the sixteenth-century: *fokkinge*, *krappe* and *buggere*.

The pantomime is Britain's home-grown Christmas spectacular. Only British audiences enjoy the barrage of sexual jokes and double entendres, the sight of a television personality taking a turn as the 'principal boy' (usually, a cross-dressed weather girl) or the 'dame' (the beefcake with the hairy back from the house and garden show). Only British audiences

know when to yell at the stage, 'He's behind you!' and delight in the incredulous response, then howl with laughter when the actor turns round and there's nobody there. A case of little things pleasing little minds, perhaps?

> *'The British public has always had an unerring taste for ungifted amateurs.'*
>
> JOHN OSBORNE

In Britain, it is borderline treason to criticize the major cultural export. But many leading Shakespeare scholars contend that Shakespeare, to quote Frank Kermode, 'wrote too much too quickly'. The poet Dryden complained that Shakespeare 'often obscures his meaning with words'. Words like appertainments, tortive, abruption, ungenitured, vastidity, and honorificabilitidunatibus. The late professor A. C. Bradley said that the Bard's language was 'pestered with metaphors' and that he sometimes makes no sense at all. 'I have felt so many quirks of joy and grief,' says the Countess in *All's Well That Ends Well*, 'That the first face of neither on the start Can woman me unto't.'

Indeed.

The Game: Britain's Sporting Passions

'FOOTBALL ISN'T JUST A MATTER OF LIFE AND DEATH,' former Liverpool manager Bill Shankly once famously said. 'It's far more important than that.' The young Lord Egremont used to be allowed by his Master of University to skip lectures twice a week to go hunting. (It was 'so suitable,' the Master said). When it comes to sport, the British lose their customary balanced perspective. Or, if it's not sport throwing life out of kilter, then it's some club or other . . . card-playing, jam-making, battle re-enacting, caravanning. The British love joining clubs. In truth, they are only truly happy in the company of people who reflect their own prejudices.

The British aristocracy have always liked their sports bloody: otter hunting, boar hunting, badger baiting, and fox hunting – memorably described by Oscar Wilde as 'the unspeakable in full pursuit of the uneatable.' The sport of goose-riding, which has mercifully died a death in recent times, consisted of trying to pull the head off a well-greased goose at a full gallop.

> *'Sport requires a certain innocence. Without innocence, the glorious inconsequentialities of sport could not exist. We demand than people take part in sport as if it were a life-and-death matter, and yet all of us, participants and audience both, know that it is all most frightfully silly.'*
>
> SIMON BARNES, Chief Sports Writer
> of *The Times*, July 2005

In 1869, twenty-one-year-old Lord Rosebery was ordered by the Dean of Christ Church to give up his racing stud – he had already entered a colt for the Derby. He refused and was sent down from Oxford without a degree. He refused to let this early setback destroy his prospects, however, and went on to become Prime Minister in March 1894.

> *'If you eliminate smoking and gambling, you will be amazed to find that almost all an Englishman's pleasures can be, and mostly are, shared by his dog.'*
>
> GEORGE BERNARD SHAW

After a late-night session, the Sussex MP 'Mad' Jack Fuller bet his drinking buddies £1,000 each that five church steeples could be seen from his home, Brightling Park, on a clear day. In the morning, he saw only four. Dallington spire was out of sight. The story goes that he built another one on the horizon, known locally as the Sugar Loaf.

Among others, the British writer and statesman John Buchan always maintained a distinction between sports and games: sports are activities in which the participant pits his skills against nature, such as hunting, fishing, mountaineering; games are competitions between teams or individuals. The last forty years have seen this distinction evaporate – almost all games are now called sports.

Cricket was recorded in the fourteenth century as one of several illegal pastimes. In 1470 anyone allowing the game to be played on his or her land faced three years' imprisonment. In 1784, the King's Bench court allowed that it was 'a manly game, not bad in itself'. Interestingly, it is said that in 1751 Frederick, the Prince of Wales (father of George III), died from injuries sustained from a blow to the head caused by a cricket ball. A delightful epigram concerning his passing follows:

> Here lies poor Fred who was alive and is dead.
> Had it been his father I had much rather,
> Had it been his sister nobody would have missed her,
> Had it been his brother, still better than another,
> Had it been the whole generation, so much the better for the nation,
> But since it is Fred who was alive and is dead,
> There is no more to be said!

ANONYMOUS

Overarm bowling in cricket was banned in 1827 after an England side was beaten by the overarm bowlers of Sussex. It was not legally reinstated until 1868.

In the nineteenth century, cricket was the game of empire. It became so popular in India that it was declared 'an Indian game, accidentally discovered by the English'. The Scots, Irish and Welsh never took to it, unable to stand still in full-length trousers for quite so long as it took to play a game, or to accept the public-school cricketing jargon, with its 'googly', 'lbw' and 'silly mid-off'.

Football developed in two ways in England, the first in which the players kicked the ball with their feet, and the second in which they picked it up and ran. The former variant was first regulated by the Football Association in 1863, and is still formally titled 'Association Football'. It was dubbed 'soccer' by its enemies (from 'Assoc.') because of the much-resented interference of the FA.

In 1588, Sir Francis Drake, hearing of the approaching Spanish Armada during a game of bowls on Plymouth Hoe, finished off his game before helping to finish off the Spanish. In the eyes of a nation committed to its games his audacious display of sportsmanship is synonymous with his victory. By contrast, in 1642 Charles I was playing golf when news of the Irish Rebellion was brought to him. He broke off his round and got down to business; a cowardly breach of sporting etiquette which had its own dire consequences in 1649 when heads (including that of the King) began to roll.

In Shakespeare's *King Lear*, one of the insults heaped on Oswald by Kent is that he is a 'base football player'.

On 1 July 1916, the first day of the Battle of the Somme, Captain W. P. Nevill, a company commander in the 8th East Surreys, presented each of his four platoons with a football, offering prizes to the first platoon to dribble and pass their way forward as far as the German front line. Needless to say, the brave (or should that be 'completely mad') commander was killed very quickly. For some reason, the British regard Nevill's fantastically stupid notion as admirable, although his and his men's heroism is unquestionable.

The Cotswolds 'Olympick' games was a yearly event in Chipping Campden, Gloucestershire, which was founded in the early seventeenth century. Among other sports, it featured shin-kicking with iron-tipped boots, for which athletes trained by beating their shins with planks of wood. The English Civil

War brought a temporary end to the games in the seventeenth century, but at the last meeting of 1652, the famous back-sword fight took place, as described in *The Last Records of a Cotswolds Community*: 'In this fight with the left hand tied to the hocks the two champions fought till one lost an eye and the other was so badly bruised that he died a fortnight after, but says tradition, it was the Campden man that won.'

The annual World Bog Snorkelling Championship takes place at Llanwrtyd in Wales. For the 60-yard swim through stinking black water, competitors are asked by the organizers to dress smart – 'no jeans, plus flippers and snorkel of course'. One can therefore imagine burly Welsh bouncers turning away inadequately attired bog-snorkellers with a condescending sneer.

Every year the Hare Pie Scramble and Bottle Kicking takes place on Easter Monday in the Leicestershire village of Hallaton. Its eighteenth-century origins lie in a gift of land made to the rector on condition that he provided two hare pies and a quantity of ale to be scrambled for by the poor. The Scramble goes on by the church gate. The Bottle Kicking is played by two teams using three small, iron-hooped, wooden barrels (the 'bottles'). The aim of the game, which comprises three separate matches using a different bottle, is for each team to kick, carry and convey the bottle to their respective finishing lines, usually located about a mile away. There are neither hard and fast rules nor any limit to the number of team members on each side. It is not a pastime for the faint-hearted.

In 1997, thirty-three injuries during the annual Gloucestershire cheese-rolling event, including those to several spectators hit by the flying 8-pound Double Gloucester cheeses, led to its cancellation the following year. Its resumption pleased at least one local, who is reported to have said, 'If you can't hurl yourself down a steep hill after a few drinks chasing cheeses, what's the point of being British?' How true.

The Green and Pleasant Land: Britain's Countryside

THE BRITISH SEE THEMSELVES as good honest country folk, keeping a grave eye on the weather for the welfare of stock and crop, living off the fat of the land, bringing home the bacon, driving haywains through the ducksplash, eating ploughman's lunches and shepherd's pie, quaffing traditional ales in oak-beamed pubs, resting on Sundays. And if they don't actually do these things themselves, then they watch fictional television characters in *Heartbeat* doing them instead. 'And is there honey still for tea?' asked Rupert Brooke rhetorically. No, it's alphabet spaghetti, fish fingers and turkey twizzlers.

In Shakespeare's *Richard II*, John of Gaunt rhapsodizes about 'this sceptred isle', as if it were England's first privilege to be cut off from the rest of Europe. First, John of Gaunt couldn't have been less English if he had

ridden a rickety old bicycle while wearing a striped T-shirt and a beret, and with onions around his neck and a baguette wedged under his arm. Jean de Gand (or John of Ghent) was the French-speaking King of Castile and Duke of Aquitaine in France. Secondly, the 'sceptred isle' (meaning England) is only part of an isle, along with Wales and Scotland. The 'isle' in fact had *two* sceptres at the time, those of England and Scotland. Third, the 'fortress built by nature against infection and the hand of war' suffered the bubonic plague along with the rest of Europe during the reign of Gaunt's own father, Edward III, wiping out a third of its population including John of Gaunt's wife, Blanche. Finally, England took a big slap from 'the hand of war' during the reign of Gaunt's great-grandson, Henry VI, who fought and died in the Wars of the Roses. First rule of patriotism: never let the truth get in the way of a good rhapsody.

In eager Rapes and furious Lust begot,
Betwixt a Painted *Briton* and a *Scot*:
Whose gend'ring Off-spring quickly learn'd to Bow,
And yoke their Heifers to the *Roman* Plough:
From whence a Mongrel half-Bred Race there came,
With neither Name nor Nation, Speech nor Fame.
In whose hot Veins new Mixtures quickly ran,
Infus'd betwixt a *Saxon* and a *Dane*.
While their Rank Daughters, to their Parents just,
Receiv'd all Nations with Promiscuous Lust.
This Nauseous Brood directly did contain
The well-extracted Blood of *Englishmen* . . .
A True-Born *Englishman*'s a contradiction,
In Speech an Irony, in Fact a Fiction.

Daniel Defoe's 1701 poem, 'The True-Born Englishman' (from which a few lines are taken above) describes the mongrel origins of the English. Giving his inaugural lecture at Oxford University in 1870, the Victorian writer and art critic John Ruskin clearly hadn't read it: 'We are still undegenerate in race,' he insisted, 'a race mingled of the best northern blood.'

'If it is good to have one foot in England,' said the American author, Henry James, 'it is still better, or at least as good, to have the other out of it.'

In 1986 a tabloid headline read '3,000 Asians flood Britain'. When it comes to immigration, the British are back on the Churchillian beaches. Never mind that 3,000 immigrants would be hard pushed to *flood* a country of more than 55 million people.

> *'British Xenophobia takes the form of Insularism, and the Limeys all moved to an island some time ago to "keep themselves to themselves", which as far as the rest if the world is concerned is a good thing.'*
>
> The National Lampoon Encyclopedia of Humor

Dr Johnson rightly said that 'when two Englishmen meet, their first talk is of the weather.' What they have to say about it, however, is less obvious. Britain has a moderate climate with temperatures generally between 35°F and 65°F (2–18°C), rarely exceeding 100°F (38°C) or sinking below minus 18°F (minus 28°C). Against this uniform background dullness, local variations and seasonal oddities are of the liveliest interest. Interestingly, the national sports of cricket and football rely on exactly the same formula.

The London 'pea-souper' is the natural element of the Sherlock Holmes stories, as well as films about Jack the Ripper. In fact, the gothic fog – nothing but a blanket of soot suspended in freezing air – has been unavailable to villains needful of concealment and surprise for fifty years. The Clean Air Act of 1956 came after an official inquiry into the great fog of December 1952, which was responsible for 4,000 deaths, mainly from respiratory complaints. Its absence is deeply regretted by romantically inclined killers with a taste for Victorian crime fiction, and by foreign tourists.

'Before the [First World] war, and especially before the Boer War [1899–1902], it was summer all the year round,' remarked George Orwell about the curious short-circuit in the British mind which allows them to vouch for the scorching summers of old. Looked back on, the great British grey-sky events, like Wimbledon, Henley, Cowes Week, and the Chelsea Flower Show, appear in a glorious shimmering heatwave, with Union flags fluttering in the breeze,

fresh strawberries and cream, 'hearts at peace under an English heaven,' as the saying goes. Of the bitterly cold weather that often passes for early summer in Britain, the poet Samuel Taylor Coleridge more accurately remarked: 'Summer has set in with its usual severity.'

In his book, *The Adventure of English*, Melvyn Bragg couldn't escape the feeling that the English word 'foreign' sounded more xenophobic than *étranger* or *estrangeiro* of the Romance languages, or the German *Ausländer*.

'FOG IN THE CHANNEL – CONTINENT CUT OFF' ran the legendary newspaper headline. The disappointed groans of Europeans when they discovered they were stranded on the mainland must have surely been audible in Fleet Street.

Behind their well-defined coastline, the British have ready-made opinions of 'abroad' that save them the trouble of actually going there: Holland is flat; Germany is full of pine forests and grown men in short trousers; France is delightful except for the French; Switzerland has snowy mountains and excessively neat villages; Italy is hot, beautiful and chaotic. This oral tradition of travel applies equally to their own country. 'People joked about Bognor Regis,' wrote Paul Theroux before embarking on a journey round the coast of Great Britain. 'I had never been to Bognor Regis. But I joked about it too!'

Not everywhere in Britain sounds as cuddly as Woebley and Little Snoozing. Not every placename conjures up bucolic scenes of thatched cottages and honeysuckle. Some British placenames sound sinister (Grimes Graves, Grimspound, Lower Slaughter, Gravesend, Gibbet Hill, Dungeness and Bedlam), miserable (Grimsby, Blackpool, Isle of Dogs, Sunk Island), vaguely rude (Letchworth, Rutland, Pratts Bottom, Cuckold Cross and Over Wallop), or plain improbable (the neighbouring East Anglian villages of Nasty and Ugley . . . with their Nasty Boys' Choir and Ugley Women's Institute, of course).

> 'In the midst of a russet solitude, we came upon a notice board saying, "This is the City of Birmingham". There was nothing in sight but hedgerows, glittering fields and the mist of the autumn morning. For a moment I entertained a wild hope that this was really the City of Birmingham, that the town had been pulled down and carted away. Not that Birmingham had ever done anything to me. I had never been there; this was my first visit. I knew very little about it. The little I did know, however, was not in its favour . . . It made a great many articles, chiefly in metal, but so far in my life not one of these articles had gained any hold over my affections. I had never said, "Good old Birmingham!" myself, and never heard anybody else say it. In my limited experience, "Made in Birmingham" had been a dubious hallmark.'
>
> J. B. PRIESTLEY gingerly enters the City of Birmingham
> in his *English Journey*, 1933

The British town is widely viewed as a necessary evil redeemed only by the ease of escape into the surrounding countryside, or by its resemblance to the surrounding countryside. In 1889, the town of Port Sunlight, on the Wirral, was built for the workers of the Lever Brothers soap factory and featured two reproductions of Shakespeare's birthplace. The garden cities of the early 1900s used cottagey architectural designs to attract buyers, who then scratched up the hedgerows and concreted over the front gardens for off-road parking. Of the bomb-damaged cities after the Second World War, only Plymouth was rebuilt from scratch without nostalgia for the past. Its radical new street plan and modernist buildings are consequently unloved by anyone other than architects.

In a country that prides itself on its antiquity, a surprising number of placenames incorporate the prefix 'new': New Forest, New College, Newquay, Newport, Newlyn, Newtown (of which Britain has seventy-five), New Zealand in Derbyshire, and New York in Lincolnshire. Interestingly, all of the above are centuries old. In Britain, newness was evidently not always something to be downplayed.

Shakespeare's Land.

In 1801 a quarter of the English population could already be called 'urban'. By the middle of nineteenth century, England had become the first country in the history of the world to have most of its population living in towns. By the 1990s, British roads covered an area the size of Leicestershire and British car parks covered a space twice the size of Birmingham. Yet the British Prime Minister, John Major, was able to reassure the nation on the eve of St George's Day 1993 that: 'Fifty years from now, Britain will be the country of long shadows on county grounds, warm beer, invincible green suburbs, dog lovers and pools fillers and – as George Orwell said – "old maids cycling to holy communion through the morning mist".' Somebody should have told him that his rose-tinted spectacles needed a good clean . . .

The British are pragmatists, not idealists. When they try to imagine urban living they get it wrong. *Grand designs* are best avoided. In tinkering alone, they excel. For example, at the height of the urban boom in the nineteenth century, the proudest achievement of the celebrated Birmingham City Corporation was not to have built a new Jerusalem of boulevards, squares and leafy parks in the West Midlands; but in the fields of gas lighting and sanitation – a worthy piece of tinkering. In the 1960s, the City Corporation unadvisedly attempted a *grand design* by giving the city a whole new elevated road system for whizzing around in motor cars. While drivers enjoyed the utilitarian gusto of the design from their elevated ring-road, Brummies consigned to gloomy concrete underpasses were less enthusiastic. The great achievement of Birmingham City Corporation over the last twenty years has been to dismantle it all again – back to tinkering.

The English prefer to live in idealized fictional settings rather than counties. Dorset belongs to Thomas Hardy, Sussex to Kipling, the Lake District to Wordsworth and Hampshire to Jane Austen; Emily Brontë and her sisters have the moors of West Yorkshire, and Dickens has North Kent and bits of London, or indeed anywhere with a gloomy Victorian atmosphere. The Chilterns are Bunyan's 'Delectable Mountains', although only to the handful of academics who have actually read *The Pilgrim's Progress*.

British Traditions

NOTHING FORTIFIES THE BRITISH SO MUCH as an utterly pointless tradition or arcane piece of etiquette: Trooping the Colour, swan upping, barristers' wigs, ravens at the Tower of London, Changing the Guard, jabbing peas with the wrong side of the fork, and all those impressive, martial-sounding offices held by decrepit dowagers, such as Warden of the Cinque Ports.

The traditional summer horse fair in Appleby, Cumbria is a huge attraction for families who come to watch the gypsy travellers buying and selling horses, and washing them in the river. The British have a genuine soft spot for gypsies, so long as they travel in painted wagons pulled by heavy horses, and only show themselves once a year at the Appleby Horse Fair. The rest of the time their relationship is somewhat less amicable.

The Burlington Arcade in London is a covered mall of shops running nearly two hundred yards between Piccadilly and Old Burlington Street. It was built in 1818 by Lord George Cavendish, who later became the Earl of Burlington. Today, Regency decorum is still maintained by the frock-coated Burlington Arcade beadles, who enforce the ban on singing, humming, whistling, hurrying and 'behaving boisterously'. Quite how they manage the shoppers during the Christmas sales is another matter entirely.

Since 1104, the Dunmow Flitch Trials have taken place in the summer of every leap year in Great Dunmow in Essex. The Flitch Judge and Jury of twelve singletons (six males, six females) preside over the trial of a couple married for a year, whose aim is to win a flitch (side) of bacon. Under stiff interrogation and a degree of personal needling, the couple must prove their continuing devotion to each other to take home the flitch of bacon prize.

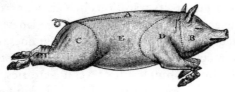

Every May in High Wycombe, Buckinghamshire, a procession of be-robed medieval dream-like figures arrives at the Guildhall led by the black-gowned beadle for the ceremonial weighing of the town's outgoing mayor. In a sonorous voice, the beadle proclaims the mayoral weight. Dressed in red and black robes, and sporting the official chain of office, he or she must not be heavier than the year before to avoid booing and censure from the crowd. Only if the mayor has lost weight can it have been a hard-working year.

Oxford University guards its traditions like ancient treasure. 'Nobody knows everything about Oxford University,' wrote Jan Morris in her book *Oxford*. 'A lifetime would be too short. Much of it does not mean what it appears to mean, much of it shifts its meaning from year to year, and some of it has been totally meaningless for several centuries: for six hundred years every Oxford graduate was required to swear that he would never on any account be reconciled with somebody called Henry the son of Simeon, who had murdered an Oxford man in 1242, and who was, even after so long in an unmarked grave, not to be touched with a punt pole.'

'In the end the obsession with the past gets to everyone,' writes Jeremy Paxman. 'Those who start their adulthood in passionate argument for modernization end up dreaming of a seat in the House of Lords.'

Every third week of July, the swans of the River Thames are 'upped' (counted), and the cygnets given the owner's swan mark – the owners being either the Queen, or two City livery companies, the Dyers' and the Vintners'. The annual swan upping is overseen by the Queen's Master of Swans and assisted by the Swan Keepers of the Vintners' and Dyers', dressed in red, white and blue uniforms. They travel along the Thames in traditional barges, though sometimes towed by motorboats in order to get the job done quickly.

On sunny Bank Holiday weekends, estate agents, publishing executives, accountants and marketing directors of the North Midlands – grizzled and unshaven – don their helmets and leathers and head off on glinting BMW and Harley-Davidson motorbikes to the open roads of the northern gritstone moors of the Peak District. En route they hop off in the old spa town of Matlock Bath for a cream tea and a stroll around the riverside gardens.

Since the fourteenth century, it has been the right of the Constable of the Tower of London to receive a barrel of rum from every Royal Navy ship visiting the Port of London under the protection of his guns. The Royal Navy presence on the Thames has gone, and so have the guns. But the Constable can still expect a barrel of rum each year, presented to him in a nice ceremony after a bit of parading. Any farm animals falling off London Bridge belong to him too.

Every year before the Queen arrives for the State Opening of Parliament, the Yeomen of the Guard (or Beefeaters) have a quick look round the Palace of Westminster in search of hidden barrels of gunpowder. If no terrorist plot is afoot, the Queen sends her messenger, Black Rod, to summon the House of Commons to the House of Lords to hear her speech. Every year, Black Rod has to bash his staff three times on the Commons door before being let in. Hard-won independence having been demonstrated in this way to the Queen, she can get on and read her ghost-written speech.

On Spring Bank Holiday weekend, the villagers of Combe Martin, Devon, hunt down and kill the shipwrecked traitor, the Earl of Rone, as they have done for many years for the sake of a good piss-up. Dressed in sackcloth and sitting backwards on a donkey, the treacherous earl leads a merry dance around all the pubs in the village. The villagers pursue dressed as a unit of what is now the Grenadier Guards and supported by a hobby horse with huge teeth, a jester and musicians. The earl is eventually thrown into sea.

On the second Saturday in August on the Firth of Forth, the Burry Man roams around the village of South Queensferry trying not to frighten the children and make them cry. It is a difficult task, however, because he is wearing thick woollens and covered from head to foot in burdock burrs. The furry green monster is preceded by a bellringer and gratefully sips whisky through a straw to dull the pain of the heat rash that he undoubtedly endures on hot summer days.

God for Harry!
England and St George!

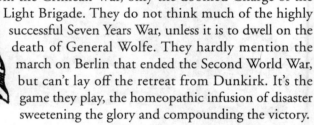

RATHER THAN GLORIFY THEIR MILITARY PAST, the British like to pretend it was always a near-run thing. They do not remember the victories from the Crimean War, only the doomed Charge of the Light Brigade. They do not think much of the highly successful Seven Years War, unless it is to dwell on the death of General Wolfe. They hardly mention the march on Berlin that ended the Second World War, but can't lay off the retreat from Dunkirk. It's the game they play, the homeopathic infusion of disaster sweetening the glory and compounding the victory.

The British thank their leaders only for *winning* battles. Good kings are the lion-hearted Richard I (who beat the Saracens), Henry V (who beat the French), Henry VIII (who beat the Pope), and Elizabeth I (who beat the Spanish Armada). Bad kings are John (who lost Normandy), Edward II (who lost Scotland), Richard III (who lost his throne), 'Bloody Mary' (who lost Calais), and 'mad' George III (who lost America). British monarchs and warlords must be victorious and infallible. If they can die in the field, then all the better.

The English expression 'to soldier on' doesn't mean to march briskly to a certain victory around the corner, it means to show plodding resilience in spite of impending physical collapse. War is never looked for by the British. When it comes, the Brits are always the underdogs, whose victories are hard fought, whose campaigns are muddy and laborious, whose losses are gallant and inevitable. 'We don't want to fight, But by jingo if we do,' rang the chorus of a popular musical-hall song . . .

In 1870, some years after the Crimean War, reforms ensured that all officers underwent formal military training. Until then, glory-seeking officers had blundered into the army with commissions they had bought (or which had been bought for them). Nevertheless, the cavalry catastrophe at Balaclava in 1854 was vigorously celebrated by the Victorian Poet Laureate Alfred Tennyson. While his poem 'The Charge of the Light Brigade' admits that 'Someone had blunder'd,' the blunder is seen as the

perfect opportunity for a display of reckless
heroism, a British forte much admired on the
cricket pitches of Victorian public schools,
though not necessarily a good idea on the
battlefield. Two very successful British actions
on the same day as the Light Brigade's charge
– the charge of the Heavy Brigade, and the
infantry action in which a battalion of
Highlanders won fame as the 'Thin Red Line' –
somehow never quite gained the same celebrity
among the disaster-loving British public.

The eighteenth century is remembered as the Age of Enlightenment, but
it was also the age of incessant wars. Queen Anne's reign (1702–14) was
almost entirely taken up by the War of the Spanish Succession. Then the
War of the Austrian Succession broke out in 1739. Followed by the Seven
Years' War (1756–63) against France and the American Revolution
(1775–83), followed by the Napoleonic Wars (1800–15) against France
(again). The War of Jenkins's Ear (1739–42) against Spain is chiefly
remembered for its silly-sounding name. (Jenkins was a British sea captain
whose ear was struck off when his ship was boarded by Spanish forces. The
ear was later produced in Britain as evidence of the dastardly nature and
general foreign-ness of the Spaniards.)

Henry V's triumph over the French at Agincourt in 1415 is fêted as one of the greatest victories in British military history. Key to the English triumph was being vastly outnumbered by the French. The first account of the battle, written three years afterwards by a clergyman who fought with Henry, said the French had 'thirty times as many' as the English. By the time Shakespeare was writing *Henry V*, estimates of French superiority (in numbers) had been scaled down to ten to one. For the last fifty years, historians have fixed on four to one. New research into the original enrolment records now has it at three to two.

The poet John Freeman commemorated the outbreak of the First World War in August 1914 with the patriotic line, 'There is not anything more wonderful Than a great people moving towards the deep Of an unguessed and unfeared future.' Freeman was unfortunately prevented from moving towards the recruiting office by a weak heart. The poet Charles Hamilton Sorley (who served as an infantry officer and was killed in action in 1915) saw himself as the lone voice of unsentimentality. 'I'm thankful to see that Kipling hasn't written a poem yet,' he said wryly. Rupert Brooke, he judged, 'is far too obsessed with his own sacrifice'. His own poem 'All the hills and vales along', written in September 1914, he felt deserved a prize not for being good, but 'for being the first poem written since 4 August that isn't patriotic':

> All the hills and vales along
> Earth is bursting into song,
> And the singers are the chaps
> Who are going to die perhaps.
> O sing, marching men,
> Till the valleys ring again.
> Give your gladness to earth's keeping,
> So be glad, when you are sleeping.
>
> Earth that never doubts nor fears,
> Earth that knows of death, not tears,
> Earth that bore with joyful ease
> Hemlock for Socrates,
> Earth that blossomed and was glad
> 'Neath the cross that Christ had,
> Shall rejoice and blossom too
> When the bullet reaches you.
> Wherefore, men marching

On the road to death, sing!
Pour gladness on earth's head,
So be merry, so be dead.

The least successful admiral of a British fleet was Sir Cloudesley Shovell. A safe pair of hands in battle, he was considered lethal outside the theatre of war. His loss of 2,000 sailors – half of the British naval fleet he was commanding – on the Goodwin Sands off Kent in a storm in 1703 was the biggest disaster up to that time in the history of the Royal Navy at peace or war. He smashed another fleet into the Scilly Isles in October 1707 on its way back from the Mediterranean, where they had been fighting the War of the Spanish Succession, with the loss of four ships and hundreds of sailors. Sir Cloudesley's body was washed up on a rock, and was found to have been robbed by wreckers, a fine old tradition in that corner of Britain.

The display of English courage against the Viking enemy in Essex, in 991, has given the Anglo-Saxon poem 'The Battle of Maldon' classic status. Saxon alderman Byrhtnoth's tactic of letting the seaborne enemy regroup on the shore is perhaps the first recorded example of English fair play. His defiant speech (below) might equally have come out of Churchill's mouth a thousand years later.

> Here stands an earl undaunted with his troop,
> One who intends to save this fatherland,
> Ethelred's kingdom, and my life lord's land
> And people. It seems to me too shameful
> That you should take our tribute to your ships
> Without a fight, now that you have advanced
> So far on to our soil. You shall not win
> Treasure so easily; but spear and sword
> Must first decide between us, the grim sport
> Of war, before we pay tribute to you.

What happened next was that the Vikings killed Byrhtnoth and trounced his Saxons, leading to a period of Danish conquest. There is nothing like an epic defeat to stir the poetic soul of the English.

Church and State

THE BRITISH STATE IS FULL OF ITS OWN LIBERAL-MINDEDNESS. How it loves to dwell on the march of progress. But British freedoms have typically been won in spite of governments, not because of them. Nevertheless, the antics of slippery, barbaric, self-serving governments afford the British people a fund of good stories. Like the one about Henry VIII making *himself* head of the English Church (which he founded for the purpose) for a quick divorce and a ton of cash. Still, the Church of England has mellowed into the perfect religion for a pragmatic nation. For the use of its facilities at baptisms, marriages and funerals, it requires only a vague belief in God (just in the 'there's-something-out-there' sense), a vaguer belief in Christ (merely as a great guy with a strong humanist message), but a strong, heartfelt commitment to BBC television on Sunday afternoons (*Songs of Praise* and *The Vicar of Dibley*).

The great eighteenth-century politician and Prime Minister William Pitt the Elder died in high patriotic fashion after collapsing in the middle of a stirring speech denouncing American independence. He began his political career with less fanfare, elected to Parliament as the member for the 'rotten borough' of Old Sarum, an old Wiltshire town consisting only of the ruins of a Norman castle, a small population of rabbits, and an even tinier one of voters.

THE KING IS DEAD! LONG LIVE THE KING!

1066   William of Normandy shoots Harold in the eye (possibly . . .) and becomes King of England.

1100   William II is accidentally-on-purpose shot while out hunting. His brother quickly becomes king.

1216   King John dies of gut rot after eating too many plums in Newark Castle while on the warpath against the barons who made him sign the Magna Carta.

1327   Edward II is murdered on the orders of his French wife Isabella and her lover Roger Mortimer by the insertion of a red-hot poker up his arse. (This was a kind of off-colour upper-class joke, for Edward was gay.) His bloodcurdling screams can still be heard echoing round the Gloucestershire castle where he died, but only by cats and dogs.

1399   Richard II is starved to death at Pontefract by his successor, Henry IV.

1422   Henry V dies of dysentery caught from the disease-ridden French town he is besieging. His six-month-old son Henry VI is left to take up the slack.

1471   Henry VI is bumped off during the Wars of the Roses on the orders of his son, the about-to-be King Edward IV.

1483   The boy-king Edward V and his younger brother are suffocated in the Tower of London on their uncle Richard of York's orders. The latter becomes King Richard III.

1553   Lady Jane 'queen for nine days' Grey is executed on her successor's orders. She sees her husband's decapitated body carried past her cell.

1649   Charles I is beheaded outside the Banqueting House in Whitehall on the orders of Parliament. His last words, that 'a subject and sovereign are clean different things,' ring true at once, the latter being a head shorter than the former.

Parliament's Act of Settlement in 1701 prevented a Catholic monarch from taking the throne, Catholics being seen as kilt-wearing Jacobites intent on reversing the Protestant Reformation, making alliances with

England's traditional enemies in Europe, and generally behaving abominably. When Queen Anne died in 1714, predeceased by all seventeen of her children, the Elector of Hanover, a German prince, acceded to the British throne as George I. Fifty-seven candidates had a better claim. The Act is still in force.

THE FINAL YEAR FOR SOME THE BEST-LOVED CRIMES AGAINST BRITISH HUMANITY:

1860   Sodomy still carries the death penalty.
1881   Married women have absolutely no property rights.
1910   The unelected House of Lords can veto House of Commons legislation.
1927   Women still can't vote.
1966   Abortion is illegal.
1959   *Lady Chatterley's Lover* is unavailable to the British public.
1968   Divorce requires a guilty party, and evidence – usually of adultery – too. (Private detective agencies do a roaring business.)
1975   Employers are free to discriminate on the grounds of gender.
1991   Women priests are barred from the Church of England.

The idea that running the country was a part-time job like running an estate persisted into the mid-nineteenth century. Britain's first 'professional' Prime Minister, Benjamin Disraeli, cut an unconventional figure in the Conservative Party, yet he wanted nothing more than to blend harmoniously into the Anglican squirearchy. In no time at all, the Jewish literary dandy (the family's name was originally d'Israeli) had set himself up as an English country gentleman in a nice big Buckinghamshire estate, and he eventually slipped into the House of Lords as the Earl of Beaconsfield.

Deep down, the arrival of Christianity in Britain so long after Christ's death is a disappointment to patriotic British Christians. The failure of history, however, is the opportunity of British legend. According to one such legend, Christ Himself came to Britain as a boy, and shortly after His crucifixion, the first Christian church was built at Glastonbury by Joseph of Arimathea in *c.*37. To many British people, it seems a divine oversight that Christ did not live in the West Country.

A law passed in 1313 to ensure parliamentary debates were conducted peaceably is still in force today. According to this law, MPs are forbidden to wear armour in Parliament.

Back in the sixteenth century, William Tyndale smuggled the first copies of his revolutionary English-language New Testament – the first bible to be made available for reading by ordinary people; that is, people who couldn't read Latin or Greek (of course, a very large number of people then couldn't read at all) – into England from Germany. Like a good repressive monarch, Henry VIII ordered his navy's ships to stop and search boats and confiscate as many bibles as possible. Finally, the Bishop of London bought every remaining copy from Tyndale, and burned the lot. Tyndale ploughed the bishop's money into a larger print run and began his second and more successful smuggling campaign; his translations later formed the basis of much of the Authorized Version, but he himself was burned at the stake as a heretic in 1536.

While there are fewer Muslims and Hindus than members of the Church of England in Britain, the future head of the Established Church, Prince Charles, was shot down by the tabloid media for suggesting that lottery money should be spent on mosques and temples as well as the restoration of crumbling Anglican churches.

Though churchgoing is in decline, attendance at cathedrals, boosted by tourists and concertgoers, is on the increase. St Paul's Cathedral attracts more visitors than Blackpool Tower. Heritage is the new religion.

Though not technically unlawful, dying in Parliament is discouraged. If MPs are unable to restrain themselves from dying, they must expect their corpse to be removed from the premises for the funeral. This is to avoid the expense of a state funeral, for which anyone dying in a royal palace (and the Houses of Parliament qualify as such, being the Palace of Westminster) is eligible.

'THATCHER, THATCHER, MILK SNATCHER'

Margaret Thatcher's Conservative government appalled parents of school-age children by ending the long-standing tradition of free milk at morning break. British children, however, were thrilled by the extra five minutes of playtime it gave them through not having to drink it.

1135–54   The period known as the Anarchy during the reign of King Stephen, who is in any case not taken seriously by the British on account of his unkingly name and his war with his cousin Matilda.

1441   The public execution of Joan of Arc, burnt at an English stake in Rouen, is now seen as a piece of poor judgement by the English. A more discreet dispatch in a deserted supermarket car park is thought to have been preferable.

1605–1998   Every English or British intervention in Ireland, from the Protestant Plantations to the Good Friday Agreement, went down like a lead balloon.

1649–61   The Commonwealth of Oliver Cromwell is a black spot in English history. Nobody bans mince pies at Christmas and gets away with it.

1666–7   During the Dutch Wars, the English allowed the Dutch to blockade the Thames twice, and captured two warships from their anchorage in the Medway. It's so sneaky . . . so English.

1685   The hanging of most of the population of Somerset after the Monmouth Rebellion against James II is seen as a needless waste of rope by the English. They got rid of the last Catholic King to rule England once and for all in 1688.

1746   Bearing in mind what it is like to be at an indoor Scottish ceilidh when the bagpipes strike up, 'Butcher' Cumberland's

treatment of the rebellious Highlanders after the Battle of Culloden is invariably viewed as soft.

1776–83 Britain's loss of the American colonies in the War of Independence seems a trifle negligent.

1834 Packing off the Tolpuddle Martyrs to Australia for attempting to form a trade union seems overly generous when other people have to wait months for a visa.

1956 Not many people now know why the Suez Crisis was such a catastrophe, but they are agreed it was a catastrophe.

1987 BBC weatherman Michael Fish's failure to warn of an approaching hurricane is seen as one of the most endearing moments in British forecasting history. His wacky taste in ties, however, is viewed as unforgivable.

2000 The Millennium Dome opened to a resounding question mark.

The British Class System

'ENGLAND IS THE MOST CLASS-RIDDEN country under the sun. It is a land of snobbery and privilege, ruled largely by the old and silly,' wrote George Orwell in 1941. Class has affected every aspect of British life, from politics, travel, sport, education, and law to sex. Nowadays, class has become a lifestyle choice. It is considered highly desirable to be working class or to have working-class roots. The peerage has the perk of getting out of jury service, a privilege they share with convicted felons, MPs, members of the armed forces and lunatics. The upper middle class is still recognizable by its loud and self-confident laugh. The lower middle class is the only one nobody wants to belong to.

The saying goes that rugby is a game for ruffians played by gentlemen, while soccer is a game for gentlemen played by ruffians. Partly, it's an issue of money. Until recently, top-class rugby union players weren't allowed to earn any money through sponsorship or advertising on pain of a life-long

ban. Amateurism was seen to mark them out as gentleman. In other words, only the lower classes had need of an income.

There were two classes of prostitute in British India. First-class prostitutes were reserved for British troops and required to have health checks, while local men had to make do with second-class prostitutes, who were free to spread diseases. In 1887 in the Punjab, a card-carrying first-class prostitute was fined two rupees 'for having sexual intercourse with a native'.

When Cheltenham College was founded in 1841, local residents were invited to become shareholders. But not all local residents. The invitation stipulated that 'no person should be considered eligible who should not be moving in the circle of gentlemen. No retail trader being under any circumstances to be considered.'

During the reign of Charles I of England (1625–49) a boatman over-charged his customer, and so the latter naturally raised an objection. The boatman reminded his customer of the dignity of his office by pointing to his trade-badge depicting the royal swan. The customer said the swan looked like a goose. The matter went to the Earl Marshal's Court, which fined the customer for insulting the swan. In another instance, a tailor was hauled before the same court for claiming to be 'as good a man' as his customer, a nobleman who refused to pay his bills. The court reprimanded the tailor and told him to tear up the bill.

The spies Donald Maclean, Guy Burgess, Kim Philby and Anthony Blunt proved that treachery is perfectly compatible with the values of a quintessential Englishman. Public-school- and Cambridge-educated, all four were helped through nepotism into comfortably embedded positions within the British Establishment. The art historian Sir Anthony Blunt – Keeper of the Queen's Pictures – was allowed to continue his life of privilege and academic honour for another fifteen years *after* he had admitted his treason. To these diffident, clubbable Englishmen, Stalinism was another club an Englishman might join. 'One does not look twice at an offer of enrolment in an elite force,' wrote Philby in his memoirs.

Upper-class ladies were strongly discouraged from sleeping with their servants, it being considered undesirable to have to raise the child of, say, a stable lad. Even so, the Tudor dynasty of English kings and queens had beginnings such as these. The first Tudor king, Henry VII, was the product of a love affair between Catherine of Valois, Henry V's widowed queen, and her Welsh servant, Owen Tudor. Interestingly, he was only known as 'Tudor' by the English, Tudor being the only one of Owen's many Welsh patronymics (son of Maredudd, son of Goronwy, son of Cynfrig, son of Edynyfed etc.) that they could pronounce.

The Statute of Apparel of 1363 told each class of person what to wear, and how much to spend on clothing. Craftsmen were not allowed to wear clothes worth more than £2 and their families had to avoid wearing silk, fur or silk velvet. Ploughmen had to wear a blanket with a linen girdle. Only lords were allowed to wear shoes with points more than two inches long. Only the royal family could wear gold cloth or purple silk and no one below the rank of knight could wear velvet, damask, foreign wool or sable. Anyone with an annual income below £20 caught wearing a silk nightcap got three months in jail, or a fine of £10 for each night.

Banjo Patterson's 1895 campfire classic, 'Walzing Matilda' is the song of the little man, the swagman (drifter) committing the, to the British, capital crime against the property of the squatter (farmer) by stealing his jumbuck (sheep). But the song is subversive, because the drifter is the hero, his life on the road with Matilda (his sleeping bag) a waltz, his theft of a sheep an act of independence.

> Once a jolly swagman camped by a billabong,
> Under the shade of a coolibah tree,
> And he sang as he watched and waited till his billy boiled,
> 'You'll come a-waltzing Matilda with me.'

Waltzing Matilda, Waltzing Matilda
You'll come a-waltzing Matilda with me,
And he sang as he watched and waited till his billy boiled,
You'll come a-waltzing Matilda with me.

Down came a jumbuck to drink at that billabong,
Up jumped the swagman and grabbed him with glee,
And he sang as he stuffed that jumbuck in his tucker bag,
'You'll come a-waltzing Matilda with me.'

Waltzing Matilda etc.

Up rode the squatter, mounted on his thoroughbred,
Down came the troopers, one, two, three.
'Whose is that jumbuck you've got in your tucker bag?
You'll come a-waltzing Matilda with me.'

Waltzing Matilda etc.

Up jumped the swagman and sprang into that billabong.
'You'll never catch me alive,' said he.
And his ghost may be heard as you pass by that billabong,
'You'll come a-waltzing Matilda with me.'

Waltzing Matilda etc.

The popular tale of Robin Hood reveals the British at their most confused towards the upper classes. Robin Hood started as a peasant story. The surname Hood crops up frequently in thirteenth century criminal records – either petty crooks identified with the famous outlaw or Hood was a common surname. Gradually the folk hero acquired class, and the name Robin Hood was his disguise. The Elizabethan playwright Anthony Mundy makes Robin heir to an earldom in *The Downfall of Robert, Earl of Huntington*. He sets the action in the reign of the usurper-king John, and when Richard I returns to England from the Crusades Robin has his title and fortune restored. He steals from the rich and gives to the poor. The common criminal becomes a class act.

Rude names for British posh nobs

Ra – anyone who makes no effort to disguise their public school education by adopting a fake estuary English accent. As in the posh kids in the *University Challenge* spoof in the TV series *The Young Ones*: 'Ra-ra-ra, we're going to smash the oiks.'

Hooray Henry – a general name for young posh males, most of whom are called Henry, for their habit of saying 'hooray' as other people might say 'fantastic' or 'excellent'.

Young Fogey – an under-twenty-five-year-old, almost invariably male, who shamelessly adopts the complacency of his parents, particularly in matters of attitude and dress.

Chinless Wonder – usually an ineffectual upper-class twit with a weak chin (from years of inbreeding) and few brain cells, but a loud braying voice; rarely much good at anything, let alone games.

Tim Nice-But-Dim – the name of the posh twit in Harry Enfield's TV comedy show: harmless, bumbling, slow-witted, pullover-wearing, says 'smashing' a lot.

Crime and Punishment

Almost everything has been illegal at one time or another in Britain: church-loitering, nude bathing, soot-carrying, emptying the privy in the wee hours, showing ankles in Broadstairs, blowing your nose in the streets of Newmarket, being a gypsy in the 1500s, carrying out the orders of a cat called Satan, killing the King. Although British common law is unfathomable to anyone but criminal-minded lawyers, the British have always taken great delight in the punishments, which are as imaginative as they are painful.

On 12 October 1660, Samuel Pepys wrote about witnessing the execution of one of the Parliamentarians who had pressed for the death of the former King, Charles I: 'I went out to Charing Cross to see Major-General Harrison, one of the regicides, hanged, drawn and quartered, which was done there, he was looking as cheerful as any man could do in that condition. He was presently cut down, and his head and heart shown to the people, at which there was great shouts of joy.'

> *'As a collection our statute book might be summed up as beyond the average citizen's pocket to purchase, beyond his bookshelves to accommodate, beyond his leisure to study and beyond his intellect to comprehend.'*
>
> CECIL CARR, the Chairman of the Statute Law Committee, who had the job of tidying up the laws of old England after the Second World War

On 28 January 1896, Walter Arnold of East Peckham in Kent became the first motorist to be prosecuted for speeding when he was caught doing 8 mph through the village by a traffic policeman who pursued him on a bike. Having exceeded the urban limit by 6 mph, he was fined 1 shilling.

The crimes of William Parry – courtier, spy, MP for Queenborough, rogue, and, for his part in an assassination plot against Elizabeth I, traitor – so appalled the House of Commons that it begged the Queen's permission to devise a death more excruciatingly painful and humiliating than the one prescribed by law. The Queen showed mercy to Parry by allowing him a '*normal* traitor's death': 'Thou shalt be had from hence to the place whence thou didest come, and so be drawn through the open city of London upon a hurdle to the place of execution, and there to be hanged and led down alive, and thy privy parts cut off, and thy entrails taken out and burnt in thy sight, then thy head to be cut off, and thy body to be divided in four parts, and to be disposed at Her Majesty's pleasure; and God have mercy on thy soul.'

In the new Witchcraft Act of 1604, King James I of England (VI of Scotland) banned the resurrection of corpses for 'witchcraft, sorcery, charme or enchantment' and 'making a pact with the Devil'. He then banned witches from making predictions of the monarch's death, as in Shakespeare's *Macbeth*, which was first performed in James's reign. That done, the King often took a personal hand in the interrogation and torture of witches.

In 1694, about to be deprived of his inheritance by attainder, the son of a condemned traitor seized on a loophole in the law to get the judgement overturned. The judge, he pointed out, had omitted to add that the prisoner's entrails were to be burned in front of his face in the time-honoured manner, making the sentence invalid. The Crown argued that the hanging, drawing and disembowelling of the prisoner would have finished him off anyway, and that the burning of the entrails really didn't make any difference. The son's counsel pointed to the case of Colonel Harrison, that same one of Charles I's regicides whose execution Pepys had watched, whom he alleged 'was cut down alive, and after his entrails were taken out of his body rose up, and had strength enough to strike the executioner.' The King's Bench found in the son's favour; namely that the sentence was illegal because its wording was incomplete.

The first Englishman to be executed by beheading was Waltheof, Earl of Northumberland, in 1075. The worst executioner in English history was Richard Jaquet, also known as Jack Ketch, who took four blows to behead the Duke of Monmouth in 1685, and still had to finish the job with a knife. The sobriquet 'Jack Ketch' was later attached to all those in the execution business, regardless of their proficiency with axe or rope.

Tyburn was London's most renowned place of execution. In 1196, William 'Longbeard' Fitz Osbern became the first to tread the scaffold for leading a rebellion. From 1571, there was a permanent gallows at Tyburn capable of hanging twenty-four people at a time. Criminals arrived by cart from Newgate Prison. The noose was slipped around the neck, and when the cart moved away the condemned man (or woman) was left dangling. It took about thirty minutes for the wretched victim to die from this short-drop method, during which there would be a quick rendition of the crowd's favourite, 'the Tyburn jig'. Friends and relatives pulled on the feet to hasten the process. For the sake of the squeamish, Tyburn now goes by the name of Marble Arch.

Magna Carta is the basis of English law, and the foundation of liberty in Britain, Ireland, America and the Commonwealth. But only three of the sixty clauses signed by King John at Runnymede in 1215 remain in force. The one that guarantees the rights of 'freemen' *not* to be imprisoned, outlawed or exiled without the law's say-so is still there. The one that guarantees townsmen and freemen the right to build bridges wherever they like has, sadly, been cut out.

In 1797 the inventor of the top hat, a London haberdasher named John Hetherington, was arrested and charged with conduct likely to cause a

breach of the King's peace, for 'appearing on the public highway wearing upon his head a tall structure having a shining luster and calculated to frighten timid people.'

When James I of England (and VI of Scotland, let it not be forgotten) gave his judgment on a case concerning land only to have it overturned, England's Lord Chief Justice, Sir Edward Coke gently showed the Scottish King his mistake in imagining common sense had a place in English common law: 'God had endowed His Majesty with excellent science, and great endowments of nature; but His Majesty was not learned in the laws of his realm of England, and causes which concern the life, or inheritance, or goods, or fortunes of his subjects are not to be decided by natural reason but by the artificial reason and judgment of the law, which law is an act which requires long study and experience before that a man can attain the recognizance of it.'

The House and Windows Duties Act of 1766 imposed a climbing scale of tax for houses with many windows. If you had seven windows, you had to pay 2d per window. If you had eight windows, you paid 6d per window. Nine windows, 8d per window; ten windows, 10d per window, and so on. The result was that homeowners bricked up some of their windows.

In Scotland, a condemned person suffered the ultimate insult of having to pay for his or her execution. Here is the itemized bill for the execution of Janet Wishart and Isabel Crocker, burned as witches in February 1596:

1. For twenty loads of peat to burn them   40s
2. For four tar barrels   26s 3p
3. For 24 feet of rope   4s
4. For carrying peat, coals and barrels to the hill   8s 4p
5. For one justice [i.e. magistrate] for their execution 13s 4p

The last execution for witchcraft took place in Scotland in 1722.

The author P. G. Wodehouse – creator of such quintessentially English characters as Bertie Wooster, Jeeves, and Barmy Fotheringay-Phipps – turned up on German radio in 1941 giving a series of humorous broadcasts to America about his experiences of internment at the hands of the Germans. He had been trapped in France when the country fell in the summer of 1940, and, although a non-combatant, he was interned in Germany as an enemy national. After the war, he was cleared of the capital crime of collaboration, but advised not to return to England, where forty-two Brits had suffered death sentences or imprisonment for similar crimes. Wodehouse suffered almost as harshly. He was expelled from his London club, the Beefsteak, and his old school Dulwich College removed his name from its roll of honour. Many years later, not long before his death, he was knighted, but by then he had long since settled in America, and never lived in Britain again.

In 1592, the Case of Swans explained the special status of swans under law: 'For the cock swan is the emblem of the representation of the affectionate and true husband to his wife and above all other fowls; for the cock swan holdeth himself to one female only, and for this cause nature hath conferred on him a gift beyond all others; that is to die so joyfully, that he sings sweetly when he dies.' Though it is a myth that swans sing as they die, its persistence gave the word 'swansong' to the English language.

Unicorns were not accorded the same level of protection under law, in spite of the healing power of their tears.

Until 1818, it was still possible to claim trial by 'judicial combat' in England, in the absence of direct evidence. The accused had the right to fight his accuser in front of the court. God was expected to come down on the right side. The rules specified no witchcraft, and the battle continued until dusk. If the accused was killed, his heirs were deprived of his lands and titles. If he was forced to submit, he was hanged, though with no attainder (the forfeiture of land and civil rights). In 1817, Abraham Thornton was the last person to have an appeal for a combative trial – for the murder of Mary Ashford after a village dance – upheld by the courts. His accuser, Mary's brother, refused to fight because Thornton was a big bruiser, while he was a little twerp. Thornton was freed. The following year judicial combat was abolished.

In 1406, 'peine forte et dure' was introduced for hard-cases who refused to plead 'guilty' or 'not guilty' to their crimes. Here is the precise wording of the legal definition:

> That the prisoner shall be remanded to the place from whence he came, and put in some low, dark room, and that he shall lie without any litter or other thing under him, and without any manner of garment, except something to hide his privy member; that one arm shall be drawn to one quarter of the room with a cord and the other to another, and that his feet shall be used in the same manner; and that as many weights shall be laid upon him as he can bear, and more; that he shall have three morsels of barley bread a day, and that he shall have the water next to the prison, so that it be not current; and that he shall not eat the same day on which he drinks, nor drink on the same day on which he eats; and that he shall continue so till he die or answer [to the charge laid against him].

Old-fashioned confidence tricksters:

ABRAHAM MEN pretended to be mad.
BAWDY BASKETS stole linen that was hanging out to dry.
COUNTERFEIT CRANKS feigned epilepsy, using soap to make themselves foam at the mouth.
DOMMERARS pretended to be dumb.

Freshwater Mariners pretended to be the survivors of shipwrecks.

Glimmers carried fake testimonials saying their houses had been burned down.

Hookers used poles with hooks to steal things through open windows.

Upright Men took jobs with the sole intention of stealing from their employers.

Top Ten famous literary felons:

1. **Daniel Defoe**, author of *Robinson Crusoe*, served time in Newgate Prison and the stocks for nonconformity.

2. The dramatist and wit **Oscar Wilde** spent more than a year in prison for gross indecency, and wrote *The Ballad of Reading Gaol*, where he served most of his sentence.

3. The poet **John Donne** had a spell in the Fleet Prison in 1602, aged twenty-nine, for secretly marrying a minor, sixteen-year-old Ann More.

4. **JOHN BUNYAN** wrote *The Pilgrim's Progress* in Bedford Jail, where he spent around twelve years for nonconformity.

5. The Elizabethan dramatist **THOMAS KYD** was tortured for information about Christopher Marlowe's murder, and died in poverty not long afterwards.

6. The young **CHARLES DICKENS** spent a great deal of time in Marshalsea Prison visiting his father, who was imprisoned for debt in 1824.

Charles Dickens —

7. **WILLIAM COBBETT** spent two years in Newgate Prison for an article he wrote against flogging. He emerged a public hero.

8. The actor and playwright **BEN JONSON** was jailed for killing an actor. He escaped death by reading some Latin scripture at his trial to show literacy, thereby demonstrating the clerical status that gave immunity from hanging.

9. The disreputable Warwickshire knight **SIR THOMAS MALORY** wrote *Le Morte D'Arthur* during one of his many spells in prison for theft, cattle stealing and abduction (and possibly for rape and murder as well).

10. Elizabeth I's unruly favourite **SIR WALTER RALEGH** was twice imprisoned in the Tower of London, where he wrote his swash-buckling accounts of privateering. His luck ran out after Elizabeth's death, and he was executed in 1616, during the reign of her successor, James VI and I.

In the Essex village of Hatfield Peverel, the sixty-four-year-old witch Agnes Waterhouse admitted to the Witch-Finder General that her white-spotted cat Satan was responsible for killing three pigs, a cow, some geese, and a married couple with whom she had quarrelled. A twelve-year-old witness, Agnes Brown, told the court that she had come across Satan padding across the yard with the milkhouse key in his mouth. 'Jesus!' said Agnes; the cat replied 'that I spake evyll wordes in speakying of that name.' Agnes Waterhouse was eventually hanged on 29 July 1566, doubtless rueing the day she chose to name her feline friend 'Satan'. 'Snowy' or 'Fluffy' would surely have aroused less suspicion and caused her less grief in the long run.

Afterword

S o there you have it: a fascinating summary of the strange and baffling ways of the British people throughout their long and varied history. From bloody battles and disappearing empires to quaint traditions and crazy customs, Great Britain has won and lost, risen and fallen, played the roles of both victor and vanquished, and yet the nation always manages to bounce back, whatever the cost. Unique, tenacious, eccentric, inept, bewildered: quite how we've made it this far is nothing short of a miracle.

Perhaps the last word on the subject should rightfully fall to our faithful, long-serving monarch:

> 'The British Constitution has always been puzzling
> and always will be.'
> Queen Elizabeth II